Mary Meade's
Magic Recipes

for the Electric Blender

Mary Meade's
Magic
Recipes
for the
Electric
Blender

by
Ruth Ellen Church

THE BOBBS-MERRILL COMPANY • INC.
Publishers
INDIANAPOLIS   **NEW YORK**

for

Mary and Rosemary,
Madeline and Margaret,
Betty, Adele and Marie,
members of the Mary Meade staff,
who tested, tasted or typed
to help me with this book.

Acknowledgments

The following manufacturers were kind enough to provide me with blenders to use in the preparation of these recipes: The John Oster Manufacturing Company, Waring Products Corporation, The Knapp-Monarch Company, Landers, Frary and Clark of Illinois, and The Dormeyer Corporation. My special thanks to Janet Bonnell of Oster and Helen Kyle of Waring, who were especially helpful. I am grateful to Ellen Saltonstall of the Pan American Coffee Bureau, Jessica McLachlin of the Wine Advisory Board and Marjorie Deen of General Foods Corporation for certain of the recipes, and to John Sayad, bar manager of the Ambassador East Hotel, Chicago, who advised me on the section of the book which is his special field.

Ruth Ellen Church

CONTENTS

Mary Meade's
Magic Recipes

for the Electric Blender

1

What Is a Blender?

A blender is an electrical appliance that makes daily meal preparation and entertaining less work and more fun. It takes the nuisance and clutter out of chopping, grating, shredding and mincing; it mixes or whips foods in just a few seconds; and it does something no other appliance can do— liquefies fruits, vegetables and other solid foods, thus making possible an entirely new kind of cooking.

Originally developed as a drink mixer, for turning out exotic frozen daiquiris, fresh pineapple drinks and malted milks, the early blenders were greeted with glee by healthfood fans who found they could now have their daily potions of fresh carrot juice with parsley and green pepper without going to any trouble at all. A blender will reduce even eggshells and apple cores to a liquid state, and some of the first health drinks popularized called for these ingredients.

But it wasn't long before it became apparent that a blender would do much more than mix drinks and liquefy solid foods. It was obvious the blender deserved a place of its own in a modern, well-equipped kitchen. A blender may be a luxury, but some women are beginning to regard it as a *necessary* luxury; and so will you, too, when you've really learned to know your blender.

All blenders now on the market are basically alike in that they consist of a powerful little motor in an enclosed base, and a covered container of over a quart capacity, which fits upon the base. The container is equipped with four very sharp stainless-steel blades that make thousands of revolutions per minute, cutting the food in fine pieces, pulverizing it or liquefying it, as you wish. Most blenders now have two or three speeds; all are capable of a high-speed whirlwind action, which is slowed to varying degrees by the kind and amount of food put into the container.

11

Most blenders have tops of heat-resistant glass so that you may put a froth on hot chocolate or cocoa or make such drinks as a Hot Rum Cow, a concoction of hot milk and rum. The blender cover is necessary to keep food from splashing over the sides under the terrific force of the steel propeller. One blender has a top with a removable center cap so that ingredients may be added, without splashing, to a mix in the container while the motor is running.

Blenders vary somewhat in design and construction. It is well for the prospective purchaser to examine several and watch a demonstration of each, if possible, before making a purchase. All will perform the usual blender jobs neatly, but there are some differences in design that may make one more convenient than another.

One type of blender comes apart at the base of the container so that the parts may be washed separately or even sterilized if the blender is to be used in the preparation of baby foods. This machine will operate with a Mason jar screwed into the base as well as with the conventional blender top. This makes it possible for you to prepare sauces, salad dressings and spreads in small pint or half-pint jars and to store them in the same jars.

A metal container is obtainable for another make blender. This is what bartenders use, because it gets so cold. Most homemakers prefer glass so that they can see how well the food is being mixed.

A blender with a heavy base that sits firmly on the counter while it works is preferable to one with a lighter weight base which may allow it to skid around when there is a heavy load in the container. See that the model you buy doesn't tip easily.

There's not a blender on the market that wouldn't beautify your kitchen. Without exception they are attractive in design. Some machines have bases made with different finishes, and there usually is a difference in price between an enamel finish, for example, and the more elegant chrome.

Buy a blender you'll enjoy looking at as well as using, for a blender should be out on your kitchen counter, not tucked away in a cupboard. If it is out, you'll use it half a dozen times a day—to blend the breakfast frozen juice, and the pancake mix, to whirl together a soup for lunch, and to prepare a delightful cocktail before dinner, to make the meat sauce, salad dressing and possibly the dessert. Then you can send the children happily to bed with a strawberry milk shake or an eggnog.

What is a blender? Just plain cooking *fun!*

What Will a Blender Do?

It will whirl up the finest frothy drinks you've ever drunk, from a raw-carrot-and-fresh-pineapple cocktail to a brandy eggnog.

It will turn your leftovers into smooth, creamy soups and make other soups with fresher flavors than you've ever tasted.

It will shred vegetables as you like them for salad; chop onions without tears; grate fresh coconut for a curry, potatoes for potato pancakes, and orange and lemon rinds.

It will make salad dressings so perfectly emulsified that no trace of the garlic can be found, though the flavor is evident. Watercress or parsley, capers or anchovies, pickles or cheese can be evenly blended into a dressing that won't separate.

It will chop nuts or reduce them to a nut butter. Cashew, pecan, walnut butters are new taste thrills easily made in a blender.

It will make delectable dips and dunks from cheeses, shrimp, avocados.

It will make perfect, smooth sauces. Gone forever is the lumpy cream sauce, bumpy gravy, the curdled hollandaise.

It will cut crumbs coarse for stuffing, fine for coating chops and making graham-cracker crusts.

It will make applesauce with a wholly new, really *fresh* flavor—and you mustn't peel the apples.

It will make a sherbet or frappé which you can eat right from the blender, from a mixture of fruit, juice and crushed ice.

It will mix a cake from a prepared mix in 20 seconds; one from your own favorite recipe in little longer time. It mixes pancakes, waffles, quick breads, even some yeast breads in the twinkling of an eye.

It will even grind coffee. (This practice is not generally recommended, however, because it generates so much friction heat that it might possibly damage the motor. Follow the manufacturer's recommendations on this particular point.)

It will do all these things without fuss or muss, saving utensils and kitchen clutter.

A blender will liquefy, blend, mix, chop, grate, purée, shred or pulverize food for you. What more can you ask of any kitchen appliance?

What Won't a Blender Do?

No single appliance will do every kitchen job, and a blender has some limitations.

It may not whip cream satisfactorily. You're very likely to get butter instead.

It won't whip egg whites. It will beat eggs enough for custard or cake, but won't give you volume in whites alone.

It won't crush ice without damage to those whirring steel blades. Always crush ice before you put it into the blender. Get an ice crusher to attach to a wall, or use the good old canvas bag and hammer technique.

It won't mash potatoes, but it will purée them for soup.

It won't be satisfactory for chopping meats except in small amounts for sandwich spreads. You need your ever-faithful meat grinder as well as a blender.

It won't be any easier to prepare fruits for fruitcake or large amounts of crumbs for turkey stuffing in a blender. Reason: you can work with only small amounts at a time, or the blender blades will clog. For small amounts of food the blender gives incomparable results. For large amounts, other methods often are quicker.

Does the Blender Take the Place of an Electric Mixer?

No.

A mixer will whip cream and mash potatoes; some mixers will knead bread. A mixer will take care of the bigger and the more delicate cakes better than a blender. It will handle larger amounts of foods to be creamed or beaten together.

A mixer won't liquefy solids. That achievement is the blender's alone. But with attachments it will perform most of the other duties of a blender, though not always with the same ease and speed.

Don't buy a blender *instead* of a mixer. But have them both, if you can.

Is a Blender an Economical Appliance?

In some ways you'll economize, like in using your leftover meats and vegetables in delicious soups, and eating the peelings as well as the apple.

But at the same time you'll probably be taking such a joyous interest in your cooking that you'll constantly be whirling up new sauces, extravagant desserts, delectable drinks and dunks. Entertaining is easy with a blender. You'll probably give more parties.

I wouldn't bet that there'll be any money saved at your house when you buy a blender. But you'll have a lot more fun!

How To Use a Blender

For fruit and vegetable cocktails, malted milks, daiquiris and other drinks you just put everything into the blender container (filling it not more than three-fourths full) and turn the switch. In a few seconds the carrots and pineapple juice are one, the malt, milk and ice cream are a thick, frosty delight, and the rum, lime juice and cracked ice have become that famous, slush-textured daiquiri, queen of cocktails.

When you blend solids a different technique is required. To chop, shred, grate or make a paste of solid ingredients, you operate the blender by quick on and off switches and an occasional pause to use a rubber spatula to scrape down the sides of the blender container and push the material into the path of the blades. The longer you keep this up, the finer your mixture. Coffee is an exception to this procedure; you just turn on the blender, and the coffee beans jump about until they've all been entrapped and pulverized by the steel blades. (See page 13 on grinding coffee.)

Always Work With Small Amounts

This is extremely important, especially with solids. Too much food will clog the blender blades and prevent them from operating. With liquids, three-fourths full is fine; but a heavier semi-liquid mixture slows the action, and you may not be able to work with more than one-third or one-half capacity.

Cut or break solids into pieces before adding them to the container. Break crackers or bread in, a few crackers or one slice at a time, blend the crumbs as fine as you want, pour into a bowl and begin over again. Use the same principle with chocolate, coconut, carrots, fruit—anything you want to chop, grate or reduce to fine particles.

When you switch on the blender always place your hand on the cover to avoid the possibility of a splashover and to stabilize the machine for the first impact of the blades against the food to be blended. Always be sure the container is firmly seated on the base before operating.

In making hot drinks, like chocolate, or in blending hot soups and sauces, rinse the container with warm water first, then add the hot liquid gradually. Even though the glass top is tempered to resist heat, a sudden change of temperature may crack it. Study the booklet that comes with your blender to make certain you can put hot mixtures into it.

How To Care for a Blender

Your machine probably won't need oiling. (Consult your booklet to see.) Usually all you need to do is keep it clean and treat it with respect.

Wipe off the base with a damp cloth after using. Put a little detergent and warm water in the top, turn the switch, and your blender will wash itself. Or put it into the dishpan and give it a good sudsing. Always rinse it well and dry it carefully. For cleaning, take apart the kind of container that comes apart.

Keep Your Blender Working

Keep your blender on a counter so that it will always be handy. Use it for all the good things in this book, and having learned the technique of blender cooking, go on to make your own experiments. Your blender will work hard for you, and with proper care will last for years and years.

Happy blendings!

2

Breads, Muffins,

Pancakes and Waffles

"Quick" breads can be put together so fast in the blender that you'll never believe it if you don't try it. Pancakes, especially, are mixed with lightning speed and entirely in the blender container. You can have them with chopped fruit or grated rind as easily as without. Fruit and nut breads, blender-made, are simple as counting to 10.

Remember to keep your rubber spatula handily by, for stirring down a thick mixture (*with the motor off*) when necessary. Have ingredients at room temperature when possible. Shortening or butter should be soft. I don't think you'll run into any difficulties at all with these carefully selected recipes.

BREADS—The Quick Kind

Fresh Apple and Orange Bread

(*Loaf 9½ by 5½ inches*)

Keeps at least a week.

Sift into a bowl
>3 cups sifted flour
>1 teaspoon soda
>1½ teaspoons baking powder
>1 teaspoon salt

Place in blender container
>½ cup shortening
>½ cup orange juice
>2 eggs
>1⅓ cups sugar

Blend well, then add
>1½ apples, cored, sliced
>¼ orange, including all of peel

17

Blend until fruit is chopped fine. Add and blend 15 seconds
>1 cup raisins
>½ cup nuts

Stir into dry ingredients. Bake in greased and floured loaf pan at 350° about 1 hour and 15 minutes.

Banana Nut Bread

(Loaf 9 ½ by 5 ½ inches)

Tender and rich; almost cakelike.

Sift into a bowl
>2 cups sifted flour
>1½ teaspoons baking powder
>½ teaspoon soda

Purée in blender
>2½ to 3 large bananas (1 cup, when mashed)

Add
>2 eggs
>½ cup soft shortening
>1 cup sugar
>1½ tablespoons sour milk
>1 teaspoon lemon juice
>¼ teaspoon salt

Blend smooth. Add and blend 15 seconds longer
>1 cup nuts

Pour over dry ingredients and stir lightly together. Bake in greased pan at 350° for 45 minutes or until done.

Butterscotch Nut Bread

(Loaf 9 ½ by 5 ½ inches)

Flavorsome and easy to make.

Sift together into a bowl
>2 cups sifted flour
>1½ teaspoons baking powder
>¾ teaspoon soda
>¼ teaspoon salt

Place in blender container
>1 tablespoon melted fat
>1 cup buttermilk
>1 egg
>1 cup brown sugar, packed

Blend until smooth. Add and blend 15 seconds
>½ cup nuts

Pour blended mixture into dry ingredients; mix only until moistened. Pour into greased loaf pan, bake at 350° for 45 minutes or until done.

Oatmeal Fruit Bread

(Loaf 9½ by 5½ inches)

You can't stop eating it!

Place in container
>¼ cup buttermilk
>Rind from ½ orange

Blend to grate rind. Add
>1 cup buttermilk
>½ cup cooked prunes, pitted
>½ cup cooked apricots

Blend again until smooth. Add
>1 egg
>¼ cup shortening
>½ cup brown sugar, packed

Blend a few seconds, then add
>¾ cup nuts

Blend 10 to 20 seconds. Sift together into a bowl
>2 cups sifted flour
>2 teaspoons baking powder
>¾ teaspoon soda
>1 teaspoon salt

Stir in
>1 cup rolled oats

Add blended mixture. Mix quickly. Turn into large greased loaf pan and bake in moderate oven, 350°, for 1¼ hours. Cool on rack.

Orange Date Bread

(Loaf 9 ½ by 5 ½ inches)

Wonderful flavor from a whole orange.

Sift into mixing bowl
>2 cups sifted flour
>1½ teaspoons baking powder
>½ teaspoon soda

Place in blender
>½ cup hot water
>⅔ cup dates

Switch on motor and add gradually
>1 orange, cut in eighths, seeds removed

Blend until finely cut. Add
>1 egg
>2 tablespoons soft butter
>¼ teaspoon salt
>¾ cup sugar

Blend about 30 seconds, then add
>½ cup nuts

Blend 15 seconds and turn into dry ingredients. Stir lightly and turn into greased pan. Bake at 350° for 1 hour.

Orange Graham Cracker Loaf

(Loaf 9 ½ by 5 ½ inches)

You'll enjoy this one.

Mix together in a bowl
>2⅔ cups graham-cracker crumbs*
>½ teaspoon soda
>½ teaspoon baking powder
>½ teaspoon salt

Place in blender container
>Rind of ½ orange
>½ cup orange juice

Blend until rind is grated. Add
>½ cup shortening
>3 eggs
>½ cup sugar

Blend until smooth. Add

>1 cup nuts

Blend about 15 seconds. Pour blended ingredients into crumb mixture and mix thoroughly. Pour into greased loaf pan and bake at 350° for 50 minutes.

* *About 38 crackers. You may find it quicker to crush this large amount with a rolling pin than to use your blender.*

MUFFINS—Not the ordinary kind

Banana Surprise Tea Muffins

(16 small ones)

The surprise is jelly.

Sift into mixing bowl

>1¾ cups sifted cake flour
>2 teaspoons baking powder
>¼ teaspoon soda

Prepare in blender

>1 cup mashed bananas (2 or 3)

Add

>1 egg
>⅓ cup salad oil or melted shortening
>¾ teaspoon salt
>½ cup sugar

Blend smooth, turn into dry ingredients and stir to mix. Leave lumps. Turn into greased small muffin pans. Top each muffin with

>1 teaspoon jelly

Bake at 400° about 20 minutes.

Cinnamon Muffins

(8 medium size)

Spicy and tender.

Sift into bowl

>1 cup sifted flour
>1½ teaspoons baking powder

Place in blender container
>   1 egg
>   ½ cup milk
>   ¼ cup melted or soft shortening
>   1½ teaspoons cinnamon
>   ¼ teaspoon salt
>   ½ cup brown sugar, packed

Blend smooth. Add
>   ½ cup raisins

Blend a few seconds and pour over dry ingredients. Stir lightly and turn into greased muffin pans. Bake 15 to 20 minutes at 375°.

Cranberry Orange Muffins

(A dozen and a half, medium size)

Excellent with a simple salad luncheon.

Sift into bowl
>   2 cups sifted flour
>   3 teaspoons baking powder

Place in blender container
>   1 cup cranberries
>   Pared rind of 2 oranges
>   1 egg
>   1 cup milk
>   3 tablespoons soft or melted shortening
>   ⅔ cup sugar
>   1 teaspoon salt

Blend until cranberries are chopped fine. Pour over dry ingredients and stir just to moisten flour. Spoon into greased muffin pans and bake in 400° oven for 25 minutes.

Date Nut Muffins

(1 ½ dozen medium size)

An irresistible combination.

Sift together into a bowl
>   2 cups sifted flour
>   4 teaspoons baking powder
>   ½ teaspoon salt

Place in blender container

>   ½ package pitted dates (7¼-ounce package)
>   1 cup hot milk

Let stand about 3 minutes, then blend until dates are chopped. Add

>   ¼ cup soft butter or margarine
>   1 egg
>   ¼ cup sugar

Blend about 1 minute. Add

>   ¼ cup walnuts

Blend about 15 seconds. Pour into sifted dry ingredients and mix only until dry ingredients are dampened. Spoon into greased muffin pans, filling two-thirds full. Bake in 400° oven 20 to 25 minutes.

Ginger Gems

(2 dozen small ones)

Spicy and nice with a fruit-plate lunch.

Sift into a bowl

>   1¾ cups sifted flour
>   1 teaspoon soda

Place in blender container

>   ¼ cup soft shortening
>   1 egg
>   ½ cup strong coffee
>   ½ cup molasses
>   ½ cup sugar
>   ¼ teaspoon each: salt, nutmeg, ginger, cinnamon

Blend until smooth. Turn into dry ingredients and stir lightly together. Fill greased muffin pans two-thirds full and bake at 375° about 20 minutes.

Graham Cracker Muffins

(8 medium size)

Everything goes into the blender.

Place in blender container

     ½ cup milk
     1 egg
     2 tablespoons soft butter
     ½ teaspoon salt
     2 tablespoons sugar
     16 graham crackers, broken

Blend until crackers are all mixed. (Put them into blender a few at a time with motor running.) Stop motor and add

     2 teaspoons baking powder
     ½ cup raisins or candied fruit

Blend 15 seconds longer and turn into greased muffin pans. Bake at 400° for 15 minutes.

PANCAKES AND WAFFLES—See how easy?

Batty Cakes

(8 cakes; 4 servings)

An old-fashioned treat.

Place in blender container
     1¼ cups buttermilk
     1 cup corn meal
     ½ teaspoon soda
     ½ teaspoon salt
     1 egg

Put everything in blender. Run motor until ingredients are smooth. Drop batter onto greased griddle or skillet and bake until brown, turning once. Serve with maple sirup or as an accompaniment to fried chicken.

Crêpes Suzette

(8 cakes, 2 to a customer)

Spectacular, delicious.

Place in blender container
     1 cup milk
     3 eggs
     ⅓ cup sugar
     ¼ cup melted or soft butter

      ¼ teaspoon salt
       1 piece outer rind of lemon
      ¼ cup orange juice

Blend smooth, and add gradually with motor running

      1¾ cups sifted cake flour

When batter is smooth bake one pancake at a time in lightly greased, hot, 9-inch skillet, using ¼ cup batter per pancake. Bake until brown on one side, turn and bake the other side. (Cakes may be made ahead of time and reheated with the sauce.) Spread each pancake with Suzette butter. Make this by mixing by hand

      1¼ cups sifted confectioners' sugar
      ½ cup soft butter
       1 teaspoon grated orange rind
       3 tablespoons orange juice

Roll pancakes with filling inside. Place filled pancakes in heated skillet or chafing dish and make a sauce by combining

      ⅓ cup brandy
      ¼ cup curaçao

Add 2 tablespoons sauce to crêpes, heat thoroughly and pour the rest of the sauce over the cakes. Ignite and serve flaming.

Orange Pancakes

(A dozen smallish ones; for 4)

These can be for dessert.

Place in blender container

       1 cup orange juice
      ¼ cup milk
       3 tablespoons melted shortening or salad oil
       1 egg
       3 tablespoons sugar
      ¾ teaspoon salt
      1¼ cups sifted flour
      2½ teaspoons baking powder

Switch on motor and run 15 seconds. Stop motor, scrape down batter with rubber spatula and blend again until smooth. You can pour a pancake batter right from the blender to the griddle if you like. Bake these on a lightly greased, hot griddle and serve with the following Orange Sauce.

Orange Sauce

(For 4 servings)

Place in blender container

> 1 cup orange juice
> Outer rind of ½ orange
> 1½ tablespoons cornstarch
> ¼ teaspoon salt
> ½ cup sugar

Run blender until orange rind is fine, turn into saucepan and cook until thickened and clear, stirring constantly.

Potato Pancakes

(10 or 12)

Miraculously easy!

Sift together into a bowl

> 6 tablespoons sifted flour
> ¼ teaspoon baking powder
> 1½ teaspoons salt

Place in blender

> 3 eggs

Start blender and slice in

> 6 medium-sized potatoes, pared
> 3 slices onion
> 2 large sprigs parsley

Blend until all vegetables are cut fine, then pour into dry ingredients and stir until blended. Fry in bacon drippings in a hot skillet. Serve with Applesauce (page 66) or gooseberry sauce. These are delicious. Gone is the work of grating which used to prevent many a lover of potato pancakes from making them.

Cheese Waffles

(6 large ones)

Nice for lunch.

Sift into bowl

> 2 cups sifted flour
> 3 teaspoons baking powder

Place in blender container
>   3 egg yolks
>   1¼ cups milk
>   ¼ cup salad oil or melted fat
>   2 teaspoons sugar
>   ½ teaspoon salt
>   1 cup diced cheese

Blend smooth and pour over dry ingredients; mix lightly. Fold in
>   3 egg whites, beaten stiff

Bake in hot waffle iron. Serve with sirup or as base for creamed chicken.

Pecan Waffles

Use the preceding recipe, but omit cheese and sprinkle each waffle before baking with broken pecans.

Corn Meal Waffles

Substitute 1 cup corn meal for 1 cup flour, and keep the cheese or omit it.

Chocolate Waffles

(Eight 7-inchers)

A delightful dessert.

Sift into a bowl
>   2 cups sifted flour
>   3 teaspoons baking powder

Place in blender container
>   3 egg yolks
>   ½ cup sugar
>   1 teaspoon salt
>   1½ cups milk
>   ¼ cup soft shortening
>   2 ounces unsweetened chocolate, melted
>   ½ teaspoon vanilla

Blend thoroughly, pour over flour, stir lightly and fold in
>   3 egg whites, beaten stiff

Bake in hot waffle iron. Serve as a dessert with whipped cream or ice cream.

3

Cakes and Icings

I had to be convinced that good cakes can be made in the electric blender. I used to take the know-it-all attitude that it was impossible to make a cake worth eating that way. Now I know better. Having made hundreds of blended cakes, I know that some cakes adapt to this method better than others, but that it is possible to make dozens of really fine-textured, tender cakes by the new, quick blender procedure.

The electric mixer does the bigger, eggier cakes better, and of course you can't make a good angel-food cake with a blender—it won't whip enough air into the egg whites for that. But the blender can save you much time and energy—and spare you grated knuckles sometimes, too!—on a great number of very nice cakes. Try these recipes and see for yourself.

General Method for Cakes

Have ingredients at room temperature. Use shortening, not butter, for best results. The emulsifier shortenings especially adapted for quick-mix cakes work best. Sift dry ingredients except sugar into a bowl. Put liquids, sugar, shortening and eggs into blender container. Blend about a minute, on the average, scraping down once midway, then pour the liquids over the dry ingredients and mix lightly but thoroughly.

Icings

The blender turns out butter icings beautifully smooth. Just remember not to overwork your motor with a stiff frosting. When you want a butter icing thicker than the blender will make it without wheezing a little, finish the frosting in a bowl and add the extra confectioners' sugar. Use your rubber spatula, with the blender motor off, to facilitate mixing icings as well as cake batter.

The Blender and Packaged Cake Mix

Cake mixes are simple anyway, but they're twice as easy in a blender. Here's what you do: Put ½ the liquid into the blender, then dump in the cake mix. Top with the rest of the liquid. Cover, put your hand on the top, switch on the motor and blend 5 seconds. Scrape down the batter with your good old rubber spatula, cover the container and blend again about 15 seconds. Turn the batter into your prepared pans. It's magic, for sure!

The Blender Works Fast—Watch It!

Don't run to answer the phone when a cake is in the blender without shutting off the motor. Blender blades do their mixing in a hurry, and an overmixed cake is a toughie. Remember, about a minute (time varies not only among different kinds of batter but among blenders) is all the time required before you mix the liquids into the sifted flour. Let that phone ring once more; by that time your cake will be mixed.

Applesauce Cake
(9-by-13-inch pan)
One of the finest.

Sift together into a bowl
  2 cups sifted cake flour
  2 tablespoons cocoa
  ¾ teaspoon salt
  1 teaspoon cinnamon
  ½ teaspoon cloves
  ½ teaspoon nutmeg
  ½ teaspoon allspice
  ½ teaspoon soda
  1½ teaspoons baking powder
Place in blender container
  1½ cups unsweetened applesauce (canned or fresh, page 66)

                2 eggs
                ½ cup shortening
                1½ cups sugar
                ¾ cup raisins
Switch on the motor and blend ingredients until smooth. Pour
over sifted dry ingredients and mix thoroughly. Pour into
greased and floured (or wax-paper-lined) pan and bake at 350°
for about 45 minutes. I like Coffee Icing for this.

Coffee Icing

(Will frost 9-by-13-inch loaf or two 8- or 9-inch layers)

Place in blender container and blend smooth
                3 tablespoons soft butter
                ⅛ teaspoon salt
                ¼ cup hot strong coffee
Add gradually, with motor running
                About 3 cups confectioners' sugar
Lift some of the frosting with your spatula after adding 3 cups
sugar. You may have the right consistency right there. If not,
add a little more sugar, or if the frosting seems too thick, add a
little hot water or coffee. A few drops of vanilla may be added.
Or you can flavor with rum, but the rum is better for a plainer
cake.

Banana Cake

(Three 8-inch layers)

Moist; a good keeper.

Sift together in a bowl
                2½ cups sifted cake flour
                1½ teaspoons baking powder
                1 teaspoon soda
Place in blender container
                1½ cups blender-mashed bananas (3 to 5, depending on
                    size)
                2 eggs
                ¾ cup shortening

1½ cups sugar
1 teaspoon vanilla
¼ teaspoon salt

Blend until smooth and pour over dry ingredients. Mix until just smooth. Pour into greased, floured or wax-paper-lined pans and bake at 375° for about 30 minutes. You can steal the baby's banana flakes and make an excellent banana cake when you haven't the fresh fruit. In place of the bananas use 1 small can (5½ ounces) banana flakes and 1½ cups milk. Whipped cream is the perfect filling and frosting for this cake.

Brazil Nut Torte

(Three 8-inch layers)

This one's a breeze with the blender!

Put Brazil nuts into the container a few at a time and grind fine to make

2 cups ground Brazil nuts

Turn ground nuts into a bowl. Place in blender container and beat until light

6 egg yolks
½ cup sugar
¼ teaspoon salt

Beat separately, by hand, until stiff

6 egg whites

Beat in gradually

½ cup sugar

Fold nuts into yolk mixture, then whites into the combination. Pour batter into layer pans greased, lined with wax paper and again greased. Bake in moderate oven, 350°, for 35 minutes. Put together when cool with whipped cream.

Butterscotch Cake

(Two 8-inch layers)

Café au lait *in color.*

Sift together into a bowl

2 cups sifted cake flour

> 3 teaspoons baking powder
> 1 teaspoon salt

Place in blender container

> ½ cup shortening
> ¾ cup milk
> 1 teaspoon vanilla
> 2 eggs
> 1½ cups brown sugar

Blend smooth, pour over dry ingredients and mix thoroughly. Bake in greased, floured pans at 350°, moderate oven, for 35 minutes. Cool and put together with Butterscotch Icing.

Butterscotch Icing

(Will frost 8- or 9-inch-square cake, or 2 layers)

Place in blender container

> ¼ cup (½ stick) soft butter
> 2 tablespoons hot milk
> 1 tablespoon light corn sirup
> ½ teaspoon vanilla

Add

> 1 cup brown sugar

Blend until smooth and add gradually

> About 1 cup confectioners' sugar

Blend until smooth and spreadable.

Brown Velvet Spice Cake

(9½-by-5½-inch loaf pan)

Fine texture; fine flavor.

Sift together into mixing bowl

> 2 cups sifted cake flour
> 1½ teaspoons baking powder
> ½ teaspoon salt
> ½ teaspoon soda
> 2½ teaspoons cinnamon
> ½ teaspoon nutmeg
> ½ teaspoon allspice
> 2 teaspoons ginger
> 1 tablespoon cocoa

Place in blender container
    ½ cup shortening
    1¼ cups sour milk or buttermilk
    1 egg
    1 cup sugar
Blend about 1 minute. Pour over sifted ingredients, mix well and turn into greased loaf pan. Bake at 375° for 1 hour. Cool and frost with Raisin Cream Icing.

Raisin Cream Icing

(Will frost loaf cake or 2 layers)

Place in blender container
    About 2 inches outer peeling of orange
    ¼ cup orange juice
    ¼ cup cream
    1 teaspoon lemon juice
    ½ cup raisins
Blend until raisins are fine. Add gradually, while blending
    1½ cups confectioners' sugar
Blend smooth and turn out into bowl with
    1½ cups more confectioners' sugar
Mix smooth. If frosting seems thin, you can add a little more of the sugar, but usually it "sets" a little, within a minute or so, and doesn't need more thickening.

Cinnamon Cake

(Two 8-inch layers)

This is one of the nicest of spice cakes.

Sift together into a bowl
    2 cups sifted cake flour
    1 teaspoon soda
    ½ teaspoon salt
    1 tablespoon cinnamon
Place in the blender container
    ½ cup shortening
    1 cup sour milk or buttermilk, or 1 cup milk plus
    1 tablespoon vinegar

2 eggs
1¼ cups packed brown sugar

Blend smooth, pour over dry ingredients and mix thoroughly. Spread in 2 greased, floured (or wax-paper-lined) layer pans and bake at 350° about 25 minutes. Almost any of these butter icings is good with Cinnamon Cake. Try Banana Butter Icing.

Banana Butter Icing

(For two 8- or 9-inch layers)

Place in blender container.

2 medium-sized bananas, in thirds
1 teaspoon lemon juice
2 tablespoons soft butter
½ teaspoon vanilla
¼ teaspoon salt

Blend smooth and add gradually, working it in with spatula at the last

2½ cups confectioners' sugar

Cheese Cake Supreme

(Serves 10)

Luscious, delectable, "out of this world"—there aren't enough adjectives to describe this smooth dessert!

Combine and press firmly over bottom and lower sides of 9-inch spring-form pan

¾ package zwieback, crushed to crumbs in blender
¼ cup soft butter
¼ cup sugar

Place in blender container

1 cup sweet or sour cream
1 teaspoon vanilla
4 egg yolks
½ cup sugar
2 tablespoons sifted flour
¼ teaspoon salt

Blend smooth and add in pieces

       1 pound soft cream cheese

Blend smooth, using rubber spatula as needed. Beat until stiff, then fold in

       4 egg whites

Pour over crumbs and bake in moderately slow oven, 325°, an hour or until set in the center. Cool and chill before cutting. Wonderful topped with crushed sweetened strawberries, but elegant enough plain. I sometimes simplify things by putting the whole eggs into the blender. The cake isn't quite so fluffy, but tastes equally good.

Chocolate Cake with Pudding Mix

(8-by-8-by-2-inch pan)

Easy to do and very good.

Sift together in a bowl

       1 cup sifted cake flour

       1 teaspoon soda

       ½ teaspoon cream of tartar

       ¼ teaspoon salt

Place in blender container

       ½ cup shortening

       1 cup milk

       1 teaspoon vanilla

       2 eggs

       2 packages chocolate pudding mix (the kind you have to cook to make pudding)

Blend until smooth, pour over dry ingredients and mix well. Bake in well-greased pan lined with wax paper at 350° for 40 to 45 minutes. Cool and frost with Chocolate Icing.

Chocolate Icing

(Enough for 1 square cake or 2 layers)

Place in blender container

       2 tablespoons soft butter

       1 teaspoon vanilla

2 ounces unsweetened chocolate, melted
3 tablespoons hot milk
½ teaspoon salt
Blend smooth and add gradually, with motor running
2 cups confectioners' sugar
Add a 3-ounce package of cream cheese to this mixture for a fluffy, high-piling frosting.

Devil's Food Cake

(9-inch-square pan, 2 inches deep)

Rich chocolate flavor.

Sift together into a bowl
1¾ cups sifted cake flour
¾ teaspoon salt
1 teaspoon soda.
Place in blender container
½ cup shortening
1 cup milk
1 teaspoon vanilla
2 eggs
4 ounces (squares) unsweetened chocolate, melted
1¼ cups sugar
Blend until smooth and pour into dry ingredients. Mix thoroughly. Bake in greased, wax-paper-lined pan at 350° for 50 to 60 minutes. Mocha Icing is wonderful with this cake.

Mocha Icing

(For loaf cake or 2 layers)

Place in blender container
1 package semisweet chocolate pieces (6 ounces)
¼ cup strong hot coffee (have blender container warm)
⅛ teaspoon salt
½ teaspoon vanilla
Blend until smooth. Add gradually, with motor running
2 cups confectioners' sugar

Date Nut Cake

(8-by-8-by-2-inch pan)

A moist cake that keeps well.

Sift together into a bowl
> 1½ cups sifted flour
> ½ teaspoon baking powder
> ¼ teaspoon salt

Place in blender container and blend smooth
> 1 cup pitted dates (7-ounce package)
> 1 cup strong, hot coffee (add gradually and have container warm)
> 1 teaspoon soda

Add
> ½ cup shortening
> ½ cup granulated sugar
> ½ cup brown sugar
> 1 egg
> 1 teaspoon vanilla

Blend smooth, then add and blend 15 seconds
> ½ cup nuts

Pour blended ingredients into dry ingredients, mix thoroughly and turn into greased, wax-paper-lined pan. Bake at 350° about 50 minutes. Good served warm or cold with whipped cream.

Gold Cake

(Two 9-inch layers)

Amazingly light and tender.

Sift together into a bowl
> 1¾ cups sifted cake flour
> 3 teaspoons baking powder
> ¼ teaspoon salt

Place in blender top
> 2 strips outer peel of lemon
> ½ cup shortening
> ½ cup milk
> 1 teaspoon lemon extract

8 egg yolks
1 cup sugar

Blend thoroughly, about 2 minutes. Pour into dry ingredients and mix well. Spread in two greased, floured (or wax-paper-lined) cake pans and bake at 375° for 20 to 25 minutes. Fill with a lemon filling (packaged mix, to make it easy) and frost with Lemon and Orange Icing.

Lemon and Orange Icing

(Enough for two 9-inch layers or three 8-inchers)

Place in blender container
　　Outer rind of ½ orange
　　1 strip lemon rind
　　2 tablespoons orange juice
　　2 tablespoons lemon juice
　　3 tablespoons soft butter
　　1 egg yolk
　　Dash salt
Blend until smooth and add gradually with motor on
　　About 3 cups confectioners' sugar

Graham Cracker Cake

(9-by-9-by-2-inch cake)

So speedy to make, and so good to eat!

Crumble a few at a time into the container, and blend until fine
　　12 graham crackers (1 cup, crushed)
Put into a bowl with
　　1 teaspoon salt
　　1 cup sifted cake flour
　　2 teaspoons baking powder
Place in blender container
　　½ cup shortening
　　1 cup milk
　　¾ cup sugar
　　2 eggs
　　1 teaspoon vanilla
Blend about a minute or until smooth, and add

1 cup pecans

Blend about 15 seconds to chop nuts. Pour over dry ingredients and stir together lightly. Pour into greased, floured pan and bake at 350° for 30 minutes or until done. Cool on rack and serve with whipped cream or a butter icing.

Jelly Roll

(10½-by-15½-inch shallow pan)

Impossible to make a jelly roll in a blender? Just see for yourself!

Sift together into a bowl

    1 cup sifted cake flour, minus 1½ tablespoons
    1¼ teaspoons baking powder
    ¼ teaspoon salt

Place in blender container

    4 egg yolks
    3 tablespoons cold water
    1 teaspoon vanilla or lemon extract
    ½ cup sugar

Blend until fluffy. In another bowl beat until stiff

    4 egg whites

Gradually beat into the whites

    ½ cup sugar

Pour blended mixture into dry ingredients and mix gently but thoroughly. Pour over egg-white meringue and fold together well. Line jelly-roll pan with greased wax paper. Pour in batter. Bake in hot oven, 425°, 12 to 15 minutes. Turn at once onto warm, slightly damp towel. Remove wax paper and trim crusted edges of cake. Spread with

    1 cup jelly or preserves, any kind

Roll lengthwise, cover with towel and let stand a few minutes. Remove towel and sift confectioners' sugar over top of roll. Serve Jelly Roll in slices, with or without whipped cream.

Lazy Daisy Cake

(9-inch-square loaf)

Has its own scrumptiously good topping!

Sift together into a bowl

> 1 cup sifted cake flour
> 1½ teaspoons baking powder
> ½ teaspoon salt

Place in blender container

> ½ cup hot milk (warm container first)
> 2 eggs
> 1 teaspoon vanilla
> 1 tablespoon butter
> 1 cup sugar

Blend smooth, pour over sifted dry ingredients and mix thoroughly. Bake in greased, floured (or wax-paper-lined) pan at 350° for 30 minutes.

Lazy Daisy Topping

(Covers 9 square inches)

Heat together until melted

> ½ cup butter or margarine
> 1 cup brown sugar

Add, then spread on hot Lazy Daisy Cake

> 6 tablespoons cream
> 1 cup coconut
> 1 cup chopped nuts

Slide cake under the broiler for about 3 minutes until topping is bubbly and lightly browned.

Maple Sirup Cake

(Two 8-inch layers)

*A delicate cake with a "Vermont" flavor. **Try to get butternuts for it.***

Sift together into a bowl

> 2 cups sifted cake flour
> ½ teaspoon salt
> 2½ teaspoons baking powder

Place in blender container

> ½ cup shortening
> ¾ cup maple sirup
> 2 eggs

    1 teaspoon vanilla
    ½ cup sugar
Blend about 1 minute. Add and blend 15 seconds more
    ½ cup butternuts, pecans or walnuts
Pour over dry ingredients and mix well. Bake in greased, floured
pans at 375° for 20 to 25 minutes. Cool 5 minutes, turn cakes onto
racks to cool and put together and frost with Maple Icing.

Maple Icing
(Enough for 2 layers)

Place in blender container
    ¼ cup soft butter
    ½ cup maple sirup
    ½ teaspoon vanilla
Blend smooth and add gradually without stopping motor
    About 2½ cups confectioners' sugar

Oatmeal Cake
(Two 8-inch layers)
No flour in this, but fine flavor.

Blend by ½ cupfuls, emptying container into mixing bowl each
time, until oats are cut very fine
    3½ cups rolled oats
Add and stir together
    1 teaspoon soda
    1 teaspoon salt
    1½ teaspoons cinnamon
    1 teaspoon nutmeg
Place in blender container
    ¼ cup water
    4 eggs
    1 cup sugar
    ½ cup soft or melted shortening, or oil
    1 teaspoon vanilla
Blend until smooth and add
    ½ cup nuts
    ½ cup raisins

Blend again to chop raisins and nuts, and pour over dry ingredients. Mix well and bake in well-greased pans at 350° for 30 minutes. This cake is on the crunchy side. Don't expect it to be fine textured. It's more like a torte. With whipped cream or cream filling in and on it, you'll love this dessert.

Orange Gingerbread

(8-inch-square pan)

Just a little different.

Sift into mixing bowl
> 1⅓ cups sifted all-purpose flour
> 1 teaspoon baking powder
> ½ teaspoon soda
> 1 teaspoon ginger
> ¼ teaspoon cloves
> Dash of salt

Place in blender container
> Outer peel of 1 orange, in pieces
> ½ cup orange juice
> ½ cup molasses
> ¼ cup shortening
> ¼ cup sugar
> 1 egg

Blend mixture about a minute, then pour over dry ingredients and mix lightly. Bake in greased, floured pan 30 minutes at 375° and serve warm with whipped cream or ice cream or with cream cheese softened with a little cream and flavored with a bit of marmalade.

Orange Raisin Cake with Rum

(9-inch-square pan)

Moist, orangey and luscious!

Sift together into a bowl
> 2 cups sifted cake flour
> 1 teaspoon baking powder
> ½ teaspoon salt
> ½ teaspoon soda

Mix in a separate bowl and let stand
> ½ cup orange juice
> ½ cup sugar
> 2 tablespoons rum

Place in blender container
> Outer rind of 2 oranges, cut in strips
> ½ cup raisins
> ⅔ cup sour milk or buttermilk
> ½ cup shortening
> 1 teaspoon vanilla
> 2 eggs
> 1 cup sugar

Blend until smooth. Pour into dry ingredients and mix thoroughly. Bake in greased, wax-paper-lined pan at 350° for 40 to 45 minutes. Remove from oven and pour orange-juice mixture over cake. Serve with whipped cream.

Penuche Cake

(8-by-8-by-2-inch pan)

Everybody's crazy about this cake.

Sift together into a bowl
> 1⅓ cups sifted cake flour
> ½ teaspoon salt
> ½ teaspoon soda
> ½ teaspoon baking powder
> ½ teaspoon cinnamon

Place in blender container
> ½ cup shortening
> ¾ cup sour milk or buttermilk
> 1 egg plus 1 yolk
> 1 cup brown sugar

Blend smooth, then pour over dry ingredients and mix thoroughly. Turn into wax-paper-lined greased pan and spread with meringue, piling it lightly. Sprinkle with
> ¾ cup pecans, previously chopped in the blender

Bake at 350° for 45 minutes.

Meringue for Penuche Cake

Make this by hand.

> 1 egg white, beaten stiff
> ½ cup brown sugar

Gradually beat sugar into egg white.

Plain Two-Egg Cake

(Two 8-inch layers)

A family favorite.

Sift together into a bowl

> 2 cups sifted cake flour
> 2½ teaspoons baking powder
> ½ teaspoon salt

Place in blender container

> ½ cup shortening
> ½ cup milk
> 2 eggs
> 1 teaspoon vanilla
> 1 cup sugar

Blend about a minute, or until smooth, pour over dry ingredients and mix well. Bake in greased, wax-paper-lined pans at 375° for 25 to 30 minutes. Good with Peanut Butter Icing, chocolate or whatever you like.

Peanut Butter Icing

(Covers two 8-inch layers)

This also makes an elegant ice-cream sauce.

Place in blender container

> ¼ cup peanut butter, smooth or chunk style
> 2 tablespoons soft butter
> ½ cup brown sugar
> ¼ cup hot milk (warm container first)

Blend smooth and add gradually

> About 1½ cups confectioners' sugar

Work frosting with a spatula at the last if it gets too thick to please the blender motor.

Pineapple Upside Down Cake

This popular dessert takes the same batter—it's just the Two-Egg Cake in its Sunday best.

In a 10-inch heavy skillet melt
>½ cup butter

Add and stir until dissolved
>1 cup brown sugar

Arrange over butter and sugar
>6 to 8 drained pineapple slices
>6 to 8 maraschino cherries

Pour the plain Two-Egg Cake batter over the mixture and bake 45 to 50 minutes at 350° to 375°. Loosen cake from sides of skillet with a spatula, invert on a large cake plate and serve warm with whipped cream. The same versatile batter turns into cottage pudding if baked in a square 8-inch pan 2 inches deep and dressed with lemon sauce. Or make cupcakes of it—1½ dozen of them—by baking in greased muffin pans at 375° about 20 to 25 minutes.

Snow White Cake

(Two deep 9-inch layers)

This is the perfect birthday cake.

Sift together into a bowl
>3 cups sifted cake flour
>3 teaspoons baking powder

Place in blender container
>1 cup shortening
>1 cup milk
>1½ teaspoons vanilla
>1¼ cups sugar
>½ teaspoon salt

Blend 2 or 3 minutes. This mixture is very thick. Pour over dry ingredients and mix thoroughly. Beat until foamy
>6 egg whites

Add gradually and beat until stiff
>¾ cup sugar

Fold into first mixture. Spread in greased, wax-paper-lined pans and bake 35 minutes in 350° oven. Seven-minute frosting is the usual topper for this. That you can't make in a blender. But the cake is also nice with this Apricot Icing.

Apricot Icing or Glaze
(Enough for 2 layers)

Place in blender container
> 1 cup drained soaked dried apricots
> ¾ cup hot orange juice

Blend smooth, and add gradually
> About 2 cups confectioners' sugar

Walnut Torte
(Two 8-inch layers)
A grand party dessert.

Sift together into a mixing bowl
> 1 cup sifted flour
> ⅛ teaspoon salt
> 2 teaspoons baking powder

Place in electric blender container
> ½ cup shortening
> ⅓ cup milk
> ½ teaspoon vanilla
> 4 egg yolks
> ½ cup sugar

Blend about a minute, then pour into dry ingredients and mix well. Pour into greased, wax-paper-lined pans and spread with Walnut Meringue. Bake in slow oven, 300°, for 1 hour. Cool. Put together and frost with Chocolate Whip.

Walnut Meringue
(Tops two 8-inch layers)

Beat until stiff with rotary egg beater
> 4 egg whites
> ⅛ teaspoon cream of tartar

Gradually add and beat until glossy
> ¾ cup sugar

Fold in
>1 cup nuts, chopped in blender (better do this before mixing cake to save washing container in the middle of things)

Chocolate Whip

(Very generous topping for 2 layers)

Combine, chill for an hour, then whip until stiff
>1½ cups heavy cream
>⅓ cup cocoa
>½ cup sugar

Wonder Sponge Cake

(8- or 9-inch tube pan)

The wonder is such good sponge cake for the investment of only two eggs!

Sift together in a mixing bowl
>1½ cups sifted flour
>½ teaspoon baking powder
>Dash salt

Place in blender container and run motor until these are finely chopped
>1 strip lemon rind (outer peel only)
>1 strip orange rind (all around the orange if you wish)
>⅓ cup orange juice

Add
>⅓ cup water
>2 egg yolks
>1½ cups sugar

Blend smooth, pour over dry ingredients, mix thoroughly and fold in
>2 egg whites, beaten stiff by hand (use a wire whisk).

Pour into ungreased tube pan, bake at 325° about 50 minutes, then invert cake and cool. Serve with crushed sweetened strawberries and whipped cream.

4

Cookies

Many wonderfully good cookies can be made in your blender. The cake technique—blending liquids, fat, eggs and sugar, and stirring them into dry ingredients—usually applies here, too. No creaming of fat and sugar. The time you save is considerable.

Try a few of these fine cookies, and I think you'll catch on to the way to adapt your own favorites to the blender method.

I think it's worth while to blender-chop nuts to keep on hand for use in cookies. If you chop the nuts alone, you can be sure of getting them as coarse or as fine as you want them. Sometimes they're cut too fine if you blend them along with your batter or blended cooky mixture. Slow speed on a blender that has several speeds, or quick on and off switches of a motor that has just the one high speed, will clip your nuts to bits very neatly.

Almond Cookies

(10 dozen dainty ones, 1 ½ inches across)

A good refrigerator cooky.

Place in blender container
      1 egg
      ½ cup very soft butter
      ½ cup sugar
      1 teaspoon almond extract
        Outer yellow peel from ½ lemon
Blend until creamy. Add gradually
      ¾ cup unblanched almonds
Blend until almonds are finely ground. Sift together into mixing bowl

2 cups sifted flour
½ teaspoon cinnamon
½ teaspoon cloves
½ teaspoon nutmeg

Add liquids to dry ingredients, stirring until well mixed. Form into long rolls and chill several hours or overnight. Slice and bake on greased cooky sheet 5 to 8 minutes at 350°, moderate oven. Cookies should be only faintly brown. They freeze well, baked or unbaked.

Applesauce Cookies

(4 dozen medium size)

Spicy, nutty, fruity—you'll likee!

Chop coarse in blender and place in mixing bowl
1 cup nuts
Add
1 cup raisins
2½ cups sifted flour
1 teaspoon soda
½ teaspoon salt
½ teaspoon cinnamon
½ teaspoon cloves
½ teaspoon nutmeg
Place in blender container
½ cup shortening
1 egg
1 cup thick applesauce
1 cup sugar

Blend smooth and turn into flour mixture. Mix with spoon and drop by spoonfuls on greased cooky sheet, allowing 2 inches between cookies. Bake in moderate oven, 350°, about 15 to 20 minutes or until browned.

Banana Oatmeal Cookies

(4 dozen)
Delicious and so easy!

Place in blender container

> ¾ cup shortening
> 1 cup sugar
> 1 egg

Blend until light and fluffy. Add

> 2 large bananas, cut up (or 3 smaller ones)

Blend until bananas are whipped. Add

> ½ cup pecans or walnuts

Blend a few seconds until nuts are coarsely chopped. Sift together into mixing bowl

> 1½ cups sifted flour
> 1 teaspoon salt
> ½ teaspoon soda
> ¼ teaspoon nutmeg
> ¾ teaspoon cinnamon

Add

> 1¾ cups rolled oats

Pour liquid mixture into dry ingredients and stir until smooth. Drop by teaspoonfuls, about 1½ inches apart, onto ungreased cooky sheet. Bake at 400° for 15 minutes or until done.

Bohemian Butter Cookies

(About 5 dozen)

Roll these or use the cooky press.

Place in blender

> 1 cup very soft butter
> 2 hard-cooked egg yolks
> ¾ cup sugar
> 2 raw egg yolks
> Juice of ½ lemon
> Pared outer rind of ¼ lemon

Blend until thoroughly mixed and until rind is finely chopped. Place in mixing bowl

> 3½ cups sifted flour
> ¼ teaspoon salt

Stir liquid mixture into dry ingredients. Chill about an hour or until dough is stiff enough to put through cooky press or to roll in small portions. Shape as you like, or roll on floured and sugared board, and cut. Bake at 375° for 10 minutes or until done.

Brownies

(Forty 2-inch squares)

Everybody loves 'em.

Place in container
>   4 eggs
>   ½ cup very soft butter
>   2 cups sugar
>   1 teaspoon vanilla

Blend thoroughly. Then add
>   4 squares unsweetened chocolate, melted

Blend until well mixed. Sift together into mixing bowl
>   1¾ cups sifted cake flour
>   ¼ teaspoon salt

Add liquid ingredients to flour mixture, stirring well. Then add
>   1 cup chopped nuts (chopped separately in blender)

Turn batter into greased jelly-roll pan (10½ by 15½ inches).
Bake 350° for 25 minutes. When brownies are cool, spread with
Chocolate Icing.

Chocolate Icing

(A very thin coating for brownies)

Mix by hand. Combine and mix smooth
>   1 tablespoon melted butter
>   ¾ cup sifted confectioners' sugar
>   1½ tablespoons water
>   1 teaspoon corn sirup
>   ½ teaspoon vanilla
>   1 square unsweetened chocolate, melted

Carrot Cookies

(4 to 6 dozen)

Orange-speckled, spicy and chewy.

Place in blender container
>   ½ cup sour milk
>   2 eggs
>   ⅔ cup shortening

> 1 cup brown sugar
> 1 teaspoon vanilla

Blend until thoroughly mixed. Sift into mixing bowl

> 2 cups sifted flour
> 1 teaspoon baking powder
> ½ teaspoon soda
> ½ teaspoon salt
> 1 teaspoon cinnamon
> ¼ teaspoon nutmeg
> ¼ teaspoon cloves

Add to flour mixture

> 2 cups rolled oats
> 1 cup grated raw carrots (grated separately in blender)
> ½ cup blender-chopped nuts

Stir liquid ingredients into dry ones, mixing carefully. Drop dough in small balls from the tip of a spoon onto a greased cooky sheet. Bake at 400° for 12 to 15 minutes. This one's oatmealish but of a different sort.

Chocolate Bonbon Cookies
(2 dozen)

Fudgy sweets, more like candy than cookies.

Chop fine in blender and set aside in a shallow pan

> 1¼ cups nuts

Place in blender container

> 1 egg
> 1 cup evaporated milk
> 2 tablespoons shortening
> ½ cup sugar
> ½ cup sifted flour
> ⅓ cup cocoa
> ¼ teaspoon salt

Blend smooth and turn into top of double boiler. Cook over hot water, stirring constantly until mixture is very stiff, for 15 minutes or longer. Add

> 1 teaspoon vanilla

Drop from a teaspoon into nuts. Roll into balls well coated with nuts and chill until firm.

Chocolate Spice Drops

(6 dozen)

Spice and chocolate—a flavorsome duo!

Place in blender container and blend until thoroughly mixed
    2 eggs
    ⅔ cup thick sour cream
    ½ cup soft butter
    1½ cups sugar
    2 squares (ounces) unsweetened chocolate, melted
      and cooled
Sift together into mixing bowl
    3 cups sifted flour
    1 teaspoon soda
    1 teaspoon cloves
    1 teaspoon cinnamon
    1 teaspoon allspice
Add to flour mixture
    1 cup coarse cut nuts (may be chopped in blender
      separately)
    1 cup raisins
Add liquid mixture to flour and stir until well mixed. Drop from a teaspoon onto an ungreased cooky sheet and bake 18 to 20 minutes at 350°.

Coconut Drop Cookies

(4 dozen)

Tender and flavorsome; made in a jiffy.

Place in blender container
    ⅔ cup soft butter or margarine
    1 cup brown sugar
    2 eggs
    ¼ cup milk
    1 teaspoon vanilla
Blend until light. Sift together into mixing bowl
    2 cups sifted flour
    2 teaspoons baking powder

Add liquid to dry ingredients, stir until mixed and add

> 1 cup coconut (1 can moist kind)

Drop by teaspoonfuls onto greased cooky sheet an inch or more apart. Bake at 350° for 12 to 15 minutes. These are wonderful warm.

Coffee Brandy Cookies
(4 dozen)

These have a crunchy coating and keep well.

Place in blender container

> 2 eggs
> ½ cup shortening
> 1 cup brown sugar
> ¼ cup strong coffee
> 1 teaspoon brandy (or rum) flavoring

Blend well. Sift into mixing bowl

> 1½ cups sifted flour
> 1½ teaspoons baking powder
> ¼ teaspoon salt

Stir blended ingredients into flour mixture. Chill several hours. Then roll teaspoonfuls of the soft dough in

> 2 cups wheat flakes, crushed

Place dough on greased cooky sheet, 2 inches apart. Bake at 400° for 12 minutes. The coffee flavor should come through dominantly, so be sure to make double-strength coffee for these, or use 1 teaspoon soluble coffee and ¼ cup water.

Just Wonderful Chocolate Squares
(3 dozen)

A yummy brownie type.

Place in blender container

> ½ cup shortening
> 1 cup brown sugar
> 1 egg
> 2 squares (ounces) unsweetened chocolate, melted and cooled
> ½ cup milk
> 1 teaspoon vanilla

Blend smooth. Sift into mixing bowl

    1½ cups sifted flour

    ½ teaspoon soda

    ⅛ teaspoon salt

Pour liquid mixture into dry ingredients and stir until thoroughly mixed. Pour into shallow greased pan, 10½ by 15½ inches. Sprinkle with

    ½ cup nuts

    ½ cup coconut

both of which may be chopped a few seconds in the blender. Bake at 350° for 12 minutes or until done. Cool slightly and cut into squares.

Cry Babies

(Makes 6 dozen)

Keep well; good for the children.

Place in container

    2 eggs

    1 cup shortening

    1 cup sugar

    1 cup molasses

    1 tablespoon vinegar

    1 cup hot coffee

Blend until thoroughly mixed. Sift together into mixing bowl

    4½ cups sifted flour

    1 teaspoon ginger

    2 teaspoons soda

    1 teaspoon salt

Add liquid ingredients to dry ingredients, stirring until well blended and smooth. Drop from teaspoon onto lightly greased cooky sheet and bake 10 to 12 minutes at 375°. These can be frosted with a dab of confectioners' sugar icing.

Fruit Crumb Cookies

(3½ to 4 dozen)

Crisp outside, chewy within. So good!

Simmer until soft

        1 cup pitted dates
        1¾ cups dried apricots
        1¾ cups water
Place ⅓ of the mixture in the blender at a time and run the motor until you get a soft thick mass. Add 1 tablespoon lemon juice and chill. Meanwhile, sift together in mixing bowl

        2 cups sifted flour
        1 teaspoon soda
        ¼ teaspoon salt
Add
        2 cups quick-cooking oatmeal
Place in blender container
        ¾ cup soft butter
        ¾ cup dark-brown sugar
        ¼ cup light corn sirup
        1 teaspoon vanilla
Blend thoroughly. Pour into oatmeal-flour mixture to make a coarse crumbiness. Drop chilled fruit by teaspoons into crumbs and roll about until thickly coated. Place on greased cooky sheet and bake at 350° for 25 minutes.

Ginger Bars

(Makes fifty-six 1 ½ -by-2-inch bars)

Moist; a good keeper.

Place in container
        2 eggs
        ½ cup shortening
        ½ cup brown sugar
        ½ cup molasses
        ½ cup hot water
Blend thoroughly. Sift into mixing bowl
        1½ cups sifted flour
        ½ teaspoon cinnamon
        ½ teaspoon nutmeg
        ½ teaspoon ginger
        ½ teaspoon salt
        ½ teaspoon soda
Add liquid mixture to dry ingredients, stirring well until smooth.

Pour into a greased jelly-roll pan, 10½ by 15½ inches. Bake at 350° for 18 to 20 minutes. Ice while slightly warm with a thin confectioners' sugar icing flavored with lemon. Cut into bars when cool.

Gold Bricks

(20 squares)

Moist and delicious!

Place in blender container
> ½ cup soft butter
> 1 cup granulated sugar
> ½ cup brown sugar
> 2 eggs
> ½ cup sour milk
> Outer peel of ¼ orange

Blend until light and fluffy. Then add
> 1 cup pecans
> 1 cup cooked apricots

Blend until nuts are coarsely chopped. Sift together into mixing bowl
> 1½ cups sifted flour
> 1 teaspoon baking powder
> 1 teaspoon baking soda
> ¼ teaspoon salt

Pour liquid mixture into dry ingredients and stir until blended. Spread into a greased pan, 9 by 13 inches. Bake at 350° for 25 minutes or until done. Cool. Cut into 20 squares. Sprinkle top with confectioners' sugar, or serve with whipped cream.

Grandma's Filbert Cookies

(5 dozen small ones)

Very, very good, and done entirely by blender.

Grind in blender a cup at a time, until very fine, then set aside
> 3 cups filberts

Place in container

2 eggs
1 cup sugar
Dash of salt
½ teaspoon vanilla

Blend until thick and lemon colored. Add to ground nuts and mix well. Chill for at least 3 hours. Roll small portions of dough into small balls the size of hickory nuts. Place on greased cooky sheets and bake at 325° for 15 minutes or until done. While still warm, roll in confectioners' sugar.

Honey Date Bars

(2 dozen)

So simple to do, and so luscious!

Place in blender container
2 eggs
3 tablespoons shortening
¾ cup honey

Blend until creamy. Then add gradually
1 cup pitted dates

When thoroughly chopped add quickly and blend just a second or two
⅔ cup nuts

Sift together into mixing bowl
¾ cup sifted flour
¾ teaspoon baking powder
¼ teaspoon salt

Add honey mixture to dry ingredients and stir until thoroughly combined. Pour into well-greased 8-inch-square pan. Bake at 350° for 30 minutes or until golden brown. Cut into bars 1 by 2½ inches. Dip ends in confectioners' sugar. These are moist and chewy. You'll like 'em.

Lemon Drops

(5 dozen tea cookies)

You'll make these again and again!

Sift into a bowl

            2 cups sifted flour
            1 tablespoon baking powder
Place in blender container
            ¼ cup lemon juice
                Pared outer rind of 1 lemon
            ¼ cup water
Blend until rind is fine. Add
            ½ cup shortening
            1 egg
            1 cup sugar
            ¾ teaspoon salt
Blend until smooth. Pour over flour and baking powder, and mix well. Drop by level tablespoonfuls onto greased cooky sheet and bake at 400° for 8 minutes. These are tartly flavored lemon cookies, the kind everybody'll want the recipe for.

Frosted Molasses Creams

(2 jelly-roll pans full)

One of my favorites.

Sift into a bowl
            4 cups sifted flour
            ¼ teaspoon salt
            2 teaspoons cinnamon
            ½ teaspoon ginger
            2 teaspoons soda
Place in blender container
            1 cup molasses
            2 eggs
            1 cup shortening
            1 cup sugar
            1 cup warm water
Blend smooth and pour over dry ingredients. Stir and mix well. Turn into two large, flat pans (10½ by 15½ inches) and bake 15 to 20 minutes at 350°. Cool, frost with a butter icing (Lemon and Orange Icing, page 38, is good) and cut into bars. This is a large recipe and can be neatly cut in half if you like. At our house frosted creams are so popular that even two pans don't last any time at all. Children love them, and so does Papa!

Oatmeal Apple Surprises

(4 dozen 2 inches across)

No grinding of those apples this way!

Sift together in a bowl
      1½ cups sifted flour
        1 teaspoon baking powder
        ½ teaspoon soda
Add
      1½ cups rolled oats
Place in blender container
      ¼ cup milk
Slice in, with motor running
      2 apples, cored but not pared
Add
      ¾ cup raisins
Blend until chopped. Add
      ½ cup shortening
      1 egg
      1 cup sugar
      ½ teaspoon salt
      ¼ teaspoon cloves
      ½ teaspoon nutmeg
      1 teaspoon cinnamon
      2 tablespoons cocoa
Blend until mixed. Add
      ¾ cup nuts
Blend just a few seconds. Pour over dry ingredients, stir to mix and chill 1 hour. Drop by teaspoonfuls onto greased cooky sheet. Bake in moderate oven, 375°, for 12 to 15 minutes. No work at all, was it?

Orange Coconut Cookies

(2 dozen)

Nice for a tea party.

Sift together into a bowl

1⅔ cups sifted cake flour
¼ teaspoon soda

Place in blender container

1 strip orange rind (outer peel)
1 strip lemon rind
1 tablespoon lemon juice
3 tablespoons orange juice
1 egg
½ cup shortening
⅔ cup sugar
¼ teaspoon salt

Blend until mixture is smooth. Without stopping motor add gradually and blend until chopped fine

1 cup coconut

Turn blended mixture into flour and stir to mix well. Drop cookies 2 inches apart on greased baking sheet and bake 12 to 15 minutes at 350°. It's gilding a lily to frost these good cookies, but if you like golden lilies, mix a tablespoon of butter, a tablespoon of orange juice, a squeeze of lemon and a little grated rind with 1⅓ cups sifted confectioners' sugar, and top when right out of the oven.

Orange Drops

(5 dozen)

Sugar-coated and delightful!

Place in blender container

½ cup sour milk
2 eggs
¾ cup shortening
1½ cups brown sugar
1 teaspoon vanilla
Yellow rind of ½ orange

Blend until smooth, then sift into mixing bowl

3 cups sifted flour
2 teaspoons baking powder
½ teaspoon soda
¼ teaspoon salt

Add to flour mixture

       ¾ cup blender-chopped nuts

Add blended ingredients to flour mixture and stir until combined. Drop by teaspoonfuls onto greased cooky sheet. Bake at 350° for 15 minutes or until delicately brown. Remove from pan. While still hot, dip tops into icing made by combining ½ cup sugar, 3 tablespoons orange juice and 1½ teaspoons grated orange rind. Topping cannot be made in blender because the amount is too small.

Orange Peel Cookies

(3 dozen)

Candied peel and sour cream give a flavor you'll like.

Place in blender container

       2 eggs

       ⅔ cup shortening

       1 cup sugar

       ⅔ cup thick sour cream

Blend thoroughly, then add and run motor until finely chopped

       ¼ cup candied orange peel

Sift together into mixing bowl

       2⅓ cups sifted flour

       2 teaspoons baking powder

       1 teaspoon salt

       ½ teaspoon soda

Add liquid mixture to flour mixture and mix. Drop by teaspoonfuls onto greased cooky sheet, pressing small piece of candied peel into top of each cookie. Bake at 400° for 10 to 12 minutes or until delicately browned.

Sour Cream Cookies

(5 dozen fat ones or 10 dozen tea size)

Umm! Just like Grandma made!

Place in blender container

> 1 cup soft butter
> 2 cups brown or white sugar, or 1 cup each
> 1 egg
> 1 cup sour cream
> 1 teaspoon vanilla or ½ teaspoon lemon extract,
>   or pared outer rind of ½ lemon

Blend ingredients to a soft creamy texture. Sift together into mixing bowl

> 4½ cups sifted flour
> 1 teaspoon baking powder
> ½ teaspoon soda
> ¼ teaspoon salt

Pour liquid mixture into dry ingredients and stir smooth. Chill dough, then roll on lightly floured and sugared board. Sprinkle with sugar, roll in very lightly and cut cookies. Bake in a 375° oven about 10 to 12 minutes or until lightly browned.

Sugar Cookies

(9 dozen little ones)

Crisp and fine-flavored.

Place in blender container

> 1 pound very soft butter
> 1½ cups sugar
> Outer peel of ½ lemon
> Juice 1 lemon (3 tablespoons)
> ½ cup milk

Blend until well mixed. Sift together into mixing bowl

> 5 cups sifted flour
> 5 teaspoons baking powder
> ¼ teaspoon salt

Add liquids to flour mixture and stir until well blended. Round up dough, wrap in wax paper and chill. Roll out small portions of dough at a time, keeping the rest cold. Roll very thin, using as little flour as possible on pastry cloth and rolling pin. Cut with small cooky cutters. Place on ungreased cooky sheets and sprinkle with sugar—maybe colored sugar?—and bake in a hot oven, 400°, until lightly browned about 8 minutes. These are very, very good and very, very simply made by blender.

Wine Fruit Bars

(10½-by-15½-inch pan; will make eighty-eight 1-by-2-inch bars)

An excellent holiday cooky.

Place in blender container

    ¾ cup shortening

    1 cup evaporated milk

    ¼ cup port or any other wine

    1 cup sugar

    ½ teaspoon salt

    ½ teaspoon cinnamon

    ¼ teaspoon nutmeg

    ¼ teaspoon cloves

    ¼ teaspoon ginger

Blend well, then add

    1 strip outer peel of lemon

    ¼ cup candied pineapple, diced

    ¼ cup candied cherries

    ¼ cup candied orange peel

    ½ cup citron, diced

    ½ cup nuts

Blend until these ingredients are chopped. Stir into mixture of

    4 cups sifted flour

    1 teaspoon soda

This batter is very thick. Spread evenly in shallow greased pan, or about 1 inch thick on greased baking sheet. Bake in 350° oven about 30 minutes. Let cool in pan. Frost with a lemon-flavored confectioners' sugar icing and cut into bars when frosting has set.

5

Desserts

The electric blender cuts preparation time in half for many desserts and makes it easy for us to do such things as grind nuts, grate coconut and purée apricots, tedious procedures before the advent of a blender—so tedious, in fact, that it often was easier to select another recipe than to make the dessert we would really have liked.

Everybody loves desserts, including me, and I find it hard not to go a little haywire in my selections for this book. After all, there must be some limitation! So you won't find here all of the luscious things that my staff at the *Chicago Tribune* and I have been able to make in the blender. But these recipes will show you how to adapt your own favorites to this new, speedy, labor-saving method.

SOME FINE PUDDINGS AND MISCELLANEOUS DESSERTS

Almond Jiffy Pudding

(5 servings)

Crunchy and good, and not at all cloyingly sweet.

Place in blender container
>   1 strip orange rind
>   2 cups unblanched almonds

Blend until finely ground. (Put ⅓ of almonds in container at a time, and empty after blending.) Combine in a bowl with
>   ½ cup honey
>   2 tablespoons soft butter
>   2 cups corn flakes

Serve with soft custard or whipped cream.

Applesauce

(About 2 cups)

The flavor is so fresh!

Wash, cut in halves and core
>   3 or 4 large apples (juicy, fine-flavored ones)

Slice into bowl containing
>   ½ teaspoon salt
>   2 cups water

(This is to prevent discoloration of apples.) Place in blender
>   ¼ cup fruit juice or water
>   ½ cup sugar (amount depends upon sweetness of
>   apples used)

Start motor and drop in apple slices a few at a time, blending until they are chopped very fine. Stop motor and use spatula once or twice to scrape down sides of container. This sauce is meant to be eaten raw, and should be eaten soon because it darkens on standing. If you prefer a cooked sauce, you can skip the salt-water bath, make the sauce and bring it to a boil. The amount of sugar to use will vary with your choice of apples. Drop 2 tablespoons of red cinnamon candies into the blender with the sauce if you like cinnamon applesauce of a nice pink color.

Apple Turnovers

(Makes 8)

An old-fashioned treat.

Chop in blender container
>   2 large or 3 medium-sized cored apples, cut into eighths
>   (for best results chop each apple separately), empty-
>   ing container after each one

To chopped apples add
>   ½ cup plumped raisins
>   3 tablespoons granulated sugar
>   ¼ teaspoon cinnamon
>   Dash salt

Prepare

1 recipe plain pastry (your own or a packaged one)

Roll pastry ⅛ inch thick, then cut into 4-inch squares. Place a large tablespoonful of apple mixture and ½ teaspoon butter in center of each square. Dampen edges with water, then fold each square from corner to corner to form a triangle. Crimp edges together with a well-floured fork and prick top of each turnover to let steam escape. Place on cooky sheet and bake in hot oven, 450°, for 20 to 25 minutes or until brown.

Apricot Bavarian Cream

(10 to 12 servings)

Looks and tastes luscious!

Place in container

> 2 egg yolks
> ¾ cup sugar
> 1 cup cooked apricots, drained
> 2 cups of juice (liquid from the cooked apricots plus water to make 2 cups)
> 1 teaspoon lemon juice

Blend until apricots are completely broken up and liquefied. Pour into saucepan and bring to a boil. Soak

> 1½ tablespoons plain gelatin

In

> ½ cup cold water

Add to hot fruit mixture. Chill until mixture begins to thicken. Fold in

> 2 egg whites, beaten stiff
> 1½ cups whipping cream, whipped

Pour into a mold and chill until firm.

Chocolate Soufflé

(6 servings)

Luncheon fare for guests.

Prepare in blender and set aside

> ½ cup fine dry crumbs (use toasted bread)

Place in container

      ¾ cup milk
      2 tablespoons flour
      2 tablespoons soft butter
      5 egg yolks
      1½ squares chocolate, cut in pieces
      ½ cup sugar

Blend until smooth and pour into saucepan. Cook and stir until thickened and smooth over moderate heat or in top of double boiler. Cool and add

      Reserved crumbs
      1 teaspoon vanilla or 2 tablespoons rum

Fold into

      5 egg whites beaten stiff with
      ¼ teaspoon salt
      ½ teaspoon cream of tartar

Bake in greased casserole set in pan of hot water for 1¼ to 1½ hours at 300°. Serve at once with plain or whipped cream or custard sauce.

Danish Apple Cake

(8 servings)

Not too rich.

Crumb in blender a few pieces at a time and empty into bowl
      6 ounces zwieback (1 package)
Mix with ¼ cup melted butter. Place in blender
      ¼ cup water
      ½ cup sugar
      1 teaspoon cinnamon
      1 tablespoon lemon juice
Switch on motor, then add gradually
      1½ pounds unpared, cored apples cut into pieces.
Blend until apples are fine. Line a buttered bread pan with wax paper. Bring paper up to top of pan to facilitate removal. Place a layer of crumbs on bottom and add a layer of apple mixture. Repeat until all ingredients are used, ending with crumb layer. Bake in a moderate oven, 350°, for 15 minutes. Cool. Chill for several hours or overnight. Unmold and coat with whipped cream, or cut in squares and top with whipped cream. This des-

sert is not overly sweet and for that reason is an excellent fol-
low-up to a rather hearty entree.

Date Torte

(9-inch-square pan, 9 squares)

Ever hear of anyone not liking it?

Place in blender container
>1 cup warm water
>1 tablespoon butter
>2 eggs
>1 cup sugar
>1 cup dates

Blend until smooth and add
>1 cup nuts

Blend just a second or two to chop nuts. Sift into bowl
>1 teaspoon soda
>1 cup sifted flour

Fold in blended mixture. Turn into wax-paper-lined, greased
pan. Bake in slow oven, 300°, for 45 to 55 minutes. Cut into
squares when cool and serve with whipped cream.

Hawaiian Coconut Pudding

(9 squares or 6 servings of pudding)

Called Haupia in Honolulu.

Grate fresh coconut in the blender to make
>6 cups grated coconut (see page 244)

Add
>3 cups hot milk and coconut water

Place in cheesecloth until all liquid is extracted. Squeeze firmly.
Coconut, which should be dry, is discarded. Place 1 cup liquid in
blender and add
>6 tablespoons cornstarch
>6 tablespoons sugar

Blend smooth and add to rest of liquid in saucepan and cook until
thick. Pour into 8-inch-square pan and chill until firm. Cut into
squares and serve. In Hawaii these squares are served on ti

leaves and eaten with the fingers. If you'd rather have a creamy pudding, use only half the cornstarch and serve in sherbet glasses. Pudding can be flavored with vanilla or rum if you like.

Lemon Cracker Pudding

(6 servings)

Simple but good!

Place in blender container
>2 tablespoons lemon juice
>Strip of outer rind of lemon

Blend long enough to grate the rind. Add
>12 soda crackers, square kind
>1 cup scalded milk

Blend until smooth and add
>1 cup more scalded milk
>2 tablespoons butter
>½ teaspoon salt
>¾ cup sugar

Without stopping motor add
>2 egg yolks

Turn into greased baking dish and bake at 350° for 45 minutes. Remove from oven and top with meringue. To make meringue, beat with egg beater until stiff
>2 egg whites

Then beat in
>¼ cup sugar
>1 tablespoon lemon juice

Return to oven for 15 minutes.

Nesselrode Pudding

(6 servings)

This lovely concoction brings "Oohs" and "A-ahs," also "Yumms."

Chop cherries in blender to make
>½ cup chopped candied cherries

Set aside and crush in blender

1 dozen almond macaroons

Add to cherries and chop in blender

½ cup nuts

Add to cherries and macaroon crumbs. Place in container

½ cup cold milk

1 tablespoon plain gelatin

Flick on and off to wet gelatin. Add

1 cup scalded milk

Blend a few seconds and add

3 egg yolks

⅛ teaspoon salt

¼ cup sugar

Turn into top of double boiler and cook until custardy. Add nuts, macaroons, cherries and

1 teaspoon vanilla

Few drops almond extract

Cool. Fold in

2 egg whites, beaten stiff

Pour into mold rinsed with cold water. Chill until firm.

Nut Pudding

(6 servings)

Velvety, cakelike texture, and so good!

Place in container

½ cup cream, heated

1 package semisweet chocolate pieces

2 teaspoons vanilla

Blend smooth. Add

¼ cup diced candied orange peel

Blend until chopped fine. Add

4 egg yolks

¼ cup sugar

Blend a few seconds and add

1 cup walnuts

Blend just enough to chop. Fold into

4 egg whites, beaten stiff

Pour into prepared pan. Bake in a moderate oven, 350°, for 30 minutes. Serve plain or topped with whipped cream.

Nut Slices

(16 servings)

Flaky pastry with a rich filling.

Pastry:
Place in blender
>1 cup very soft butter
>1 egg
>¼ cup sour cream

Blend thoroughly. Stir into
>2 cups sifted flour

Shape into 2 balls, wrap in wax paper and chill while preparing the filling.

Filling:
Place in blender
>4 egg yolks
>⅔ cup sugar

Mix until thick and lemon colored. **Add**
>1 cup walnuts

Blend until nuts are ground fine. Fold this mixture into
>4 egg whites, stiffly beaten

Roll each ball of dough on a pastry cloth into a rectangle about 9 by 13 inches. Place one piece in pan the same size. Spread evenly with filling. Top with remaining pastry. Bake at 375° for 35 minutes. Cut into bars while warm.

Peppermint Candy Pudding

(8 servings)

Easy and good.

Quarter with scissors and set aside
>½ pound marshmallows

Chop in blender and add to marshmallows
>⅔ cup pecans

Crush fine in blender peppermint candy to make
>1 cup crushed peppermint candy

Turn into marshmallow-nut mixture. Fold in

1 cup cream,whipped

Crush in blender

½ pound vanilla wafers

Line 7-by-10-inch pan with wafer crumbs, cover with marshmallow mixture and top with more crumbs. Chill overnight or for several hours.

Steamed Date Nut Pudding

(8 servings)

A fine use for stale bread.

Tear bread into coarse pieces and blend a slice at a time (empty each time) to get

2 cups bread crumbs (not too fine)

Add

1½ teaspoons baking powder

⅓ cup blender-chopped nuts

Place in container

¼ cup milk

2 eggs

¼ teaspoon salt

⅓ cup sugar

2 tablespoons soft butter or salad oil

1 teaspoon vanilla

¾ cup dates

Blend until smooth and add to crumbs and nuts. Turn into well-greased pan or pudding mold, cover tightly and steam 2½ hours. Let stand in mold several minutes and turn out. Slice and serve with Lemon Sauce, page 220.

FROZEN DESSERTS

Blender-made ice creams are exciting. No longer do you have to melt marshmallows for that velvet texture—you just blend them. The fruit is chopped or puréed, as you wish it; the nuts are chopped; the cinnamon candies dissolved without benefit of cooking. It's all so quick and easy, your dessert is made in nothing flat. Best of all, flavors are perfectly combined and smooth textures achieved when the blender prepares a dessert for the freezer.

Apple Ice Cream

(6 servings)

Fresh-apple flavor; a pretty pink.

Place in container
  ⅓ cup lemon juice
Start blender and then slice in
  3 apples, cored
Blend until smooth. Add
  16 marshmallows, soft (¼ pound)
  ⅓ cup sugar
  ½ teaspoon peppermint extract
    A few drops red coloring (optional)
Blend thoroughly. Whip
  1 cup cream
Fold apple mixture into whipped cream. Tint mixture with a few drops of red food coloring. Place in refrigerator tray and freeze at coldest temperature.

Avocado Lemon Sherbet

(4 to 6 servings)

Unusual, delightful!

Place in blender container
  3 strips orange rind
  ⅓ cup lemon juice
Blend to grate rind. Add
  1½ avocados, peeled
  1 cup milk
  ⅛ teaspoon salt
  ⅔ cup confectioners' sugar
Blend smooth. Pour into refrigerator tray and freeze, stirring once or twice during freezing. This is a pleasant accompaniment for chicken or seafood, and is a perfect sherbet to serve on a fruit plate with melon, berries and other fresh fruits. It's also nice for dessert.

Frozen Cheese with Strawberry Sauce

(4 servings)

Easy as pie, and as good.

Place in blender container
> 1 cup cottage cheese
> 1 tablespoon lemon juice
> 1 strip outer peel of lemon
> ½ cup sugar
> 1 cup dairy sour cream

Blend smooth, turn into refrigerator tray and freeze at coldest point until firm around the edges. Stir with spoon until smooth. Freeze firm. Serve in squares with saucing of
> 1 package frozen strawberries, thawed, or 1 pint sweetened fresh berries.

Cinnamon Apple Ice Cream

(6 servings)

Made with apple jelly.

Place in container
> ¼ cup red cinnamon candies (2-ounce bottle)
> ¼ cup milk, scalded

Let stand 5 minutes. Then blend until candies dissolve. **Add**
> ½ cup milk
> ½ cup apple jelly
> 3 egg whites

Blend a few seconds. Fold mixture into
> 1 cup cream, whipped

Pour into refrigerator tray, freeze to a mush, remove to chilled bowl and beat with a rotary beater. Return to tray and freeze until firm.

Cranberry Marshmallow Velvet

(6 servings)

Creamy texture, delightful flavor!

Place in container

1 9-ounce can crushed pineapple and juice
2 tablespoons lemon juice
Few grains salt
1 cup heavy cream
¼ pound marshmallows (soft)
Blend thoroughly. Then add
1 can whole cranberry sauce
Blend thoroughly. Freeze about 3 hours in refrigerator tray.

Frozen Rum and Fruit Pudding

(6 to 8 servings)

A party dessert.

Place in container
16 marshmallows
1 cup scalded milk
Blend until smooth. Without stopping blender, add in order
1 9-ounce can crushed pineapple, drained
¾ cup maraschino cherries, drained (1 8-ounce bottle)
½ cup pitted dates
1 tablespoon rum
½ cup pecan halves
Blend about 15 seconds after nuts are added. Fold into
1 cup heavy cream, whipped
Pour into refrigerator tray and freeze at coldest temperature, stirring once during process. Brandy or your favorite liqueur may be used in place of the rum. This dessert can be frozen in a tray lined with cooky or graham-cracker crumbs, and some of the crumbs may be scattered on top.

Graham Cracker Ice Cream

(4 to 6 servings)

Made quick as a wink.

Place in blender container
8 graham crackers, broken up
2 cups coffee cream
½ cup sugar

½ teaspoon black walnut or maple flavoring
Blend smooth. Break into container a few at a time
8 more graham crackers
Blend until mixed. Pour into refrigerator tray and freeze at coldest temperature to a mush. Remove from tray to chilled bowl, beat with egg beater, return to tray and finish freezing.

Oriental Marlow

(6 servings)

Spicy, smooth and unusual.

Place in blender container
1 cup milk
Dash of salt
¼ cup orange marmalade
¼ cup preserved ginger
¼ cup nuts
16 marshmallows (¼ pound)
Blend these ingredients until solids are finely chopped. Fold in
1 cup cream, whipped
Freeze in refrigerator tray at coldest temperature until firm.

Strawberry Mousse

(6 servings)

Delectable!

Place in blender container
1 pint washed, hulled strawberries
⅔ cup sugar
3 drops almond extract
Blend until smooth. Fold in
2 cups heavy cream, whipped
Freeze without stirring.

PIE CRUSTS AND PIES

I haven't found it practical to make pie pastry in a blender. Much better results are to be had the regular way. But it's fun to grate cheese or grind nuts quickly in the blender to be rolled into pastry for certain pies—cheese for apple pie, nuts for a banana-cream pie, for instance.

Any pie filling that calls for chopped or puréed ingredients can be made in the blender—at least in part. Custard types, of which our friend pumpkin is an example, are very quickly put together this way.

Crumb Pie Crusts

Nothing will ever take the place of flaky pie pastry, of course; but for some pie fillings, especially the cream fillings and the fruit chiffon kind, crumb crusts are perfect. Graham Cracker Crust probably is most popular, but cooky crusts are delectable too. For a filling that holds its shape well, ground nuts can be used as the pie's foundation. For all of these crumb crusts, the blender was heaven sent.

Don't put too many crackers or cookies into the blender at once. Break 3 or 4 into the blender, crush them fine, turn them into a bowl and repeat the performance. A flash of the steel blades and the job is done each time.

Graham Cracker Crust

16 to 18 graham crackers, blender-crushed
½ cup melted butter
3 tablespoons sugar

Combine ingredients and pack firmly over bottom and sides of 9-inch pie pan. Chill until firm or bake for 8 minutes in a moderate oven, 350°. Then chill before adding filling.

Cooky Crumb Crust

1¼ cups blender-crushed cookies (vanilla or chocolate wafers or gingersnaps)
⅓ cup melted butter

Combine crumbs and butter, and pack firmly over bottom and sides of 9-inch pie pan. Keep out a few crumbs to sprinkle over the top of the pie if you like. Chill this crust. Don't bake it. If you like, use crumbs just for the bottom of the pie and stand whole cookies up around the rim.

Corn Flake Crumb Crust

> 1¼ cups crushed corn flakes or wheat flakes (about
>   4 cups whole flakes)
> ½ cup melted butter
> ⅓ cup sugar
> ½ teaspoon cinnamon (optional)

Combine ingredients and pack over bottom and sides of 9-inch pie pan. Chill before filling.

Nut Crust

> 1 cup blender-ground pecans, walnuts,
>   black walnuts or Brazil nuts
> 3 tablespoons sugar

Combine and press over bottom and sides of pie plate. This crust clings to the pie, but doesn't hold its own shape very well. Delectable with any cream filling.

PIES YOU'LL ENJOY MAKING

Grated Apple Pie

(9-inch pie)

Super-delicious, and without a crust.

Place in blender container

> 2 egg yolks
> ⅓ cup sugar (more for apples not fully ripe)
> 2 tablespoons cornstarch
> 3 tablespoons butter
> ½ teaspoon each: cinnamon, nutmeg
> ½ cup cream

Blend just a second or two, then slice into the blender container with motor running

> 5 large juicy apples

When apples have been cut fine, fill buttered pie plate without a pastry lining. The pie holds shape without a crust. Bake at 350° for 25 minutes. Beat until stiff, using hand beater

<blockquote>
2 egg whites
½ teaspoon lemon extract
</blockquote>

Beat in, until mixture stands in peaks

<blockquote>
¼ cup sugar
</blockquote>

Spread this meringue on pie and brown in moderate oven, 350°, about 15 minutes.

Coconut Cream Pie

(9-inch pie)

Coconut flavor but no shreds.

Place in blender container

<blockquote>
1 cup milk
3 eggs
1 cup coconut
¼ teaspoon salt
3 tablespoons cornstarch
3 tablespoons flour
⅔ cup sugar
</blockquote>

Blend about 20 seconds and pour into saucepan, adding

<blockquote>
1 cup more milk
</blockquote>

Cook, stirring constantly, over moderate heat until filling is thickened and quite stiff. Keep stirring or you may scorch the mixture. Remove from heat and add

<blockquote>
1 teaspoon vanilla
2 tablespoons butter
</blockquote>

Cool and spread in baked pie shell or chocolate-cooky crust. Chill and top with

<blockquote>
1 cup heavy cream, whipped
</blockquote>

Chocolate Cream Pie

Use the preceding recipe but substitute 2 squares chocolate, melted, for the coconut. Replace a cup of the milk with a cup of strong coffee for mocha pie with chocolate.

Date Custard Pie

(9-incher; 6 cuts)

A simple dessert.

Place in blender
         1 cup pitted dates
         1 cup hot milk
Blend until smooth and add
         1¼ cups more milk
         2 eggs
         Dash of salt
         Dash of nutmeg
Blend a few seconds and pour into
         Pastry-lined pie pan
Bake in hot oven, 450°, for 10 minutes; reduce heat to 350° for 25 minutes longer.

Orange Coconut Pie

(9-inch pie)

A real palate pleaser.

Soften
         1 tablespoon plain gelatin in
         ¼ cup milk
Dissolve over hot water and place in blender with
         1 cup more milk
         ½ cup orange juice
         Pared outer rind from ½ orange
         1 strip (about an inch square) lemon rind
         2 tablespons lemon juice
         ¼ teaspoon salt
         ⅓ cup sugar
         2 egg yolks
Blend until rinds are cut fine, turn into saucepan and cook over low heat, stirring constantly, until custardy. It is really better to do this in the top of a double boiler over hot water, in order not to overcook eggs. Cool, then chill until slightly thickened. Fold in

2 egg whites, beaten stiff, then beaten with
¼ cup sugar
Pour into
Baked pie shell or graham-cracker crust
Sprinkle with
⅓ cup shredded coconut
Chill until firm.

Pineapple Cottage Cheese Pie

(9-inch pie)

A smooth filling under Pineapple Glaze.

Place in blender container
1½ cups cream-style cottage cheese
¼ cup soft butter
½ cup sugar
¼ teaspoon salt
1 tablespoon flour
Outer peel of 1 lemon
2 egg yolks
¼ cup milk
Blend until mixture is smooth and lemon rind is finely cut. Turn
into a bowl and fold in
½ cup chopped nuts
2 egg whites, beaten stiff
Turn into a pastry-lined pie plate. Bake at 450° for 10 minutes;
reduce heat to 350° and bake 40 minutes longer or until filling is
firm and nicely browned. Spread with Pineapple Glaze and
return to the oven for 5 minutes.

Pineapple Glaze

Drain thoroughly
1 No. 2 can crushed pineapple
Place in blender container
¾ cup pineapple juice
½ cup sugar
2 tablespoons cornstarch

Blend 5 seconds, turn into saucepan with pineapple and cook until thick.

Fluffy Prune Pie

(9-inch pie)

Rich stuff, so cut the pieces small!

Place in blender container
>¼ cup orange juice
>1 small piece lemon rind (outer peel)
>1 teaspoon lemon juice

Blend until rind is grated. Without stopping blender add gradually
>1 pound of pitted prunes, cooked until very soft

Blend smooth. Add
>1 cup walnuts or pecans

Blend a few seconds to chop. Pour into mixing bowl and mix in
>¾ cup sugar
>¼ teaspoon salt

Beat until stiff, then fold in
>2 egg whites

Pour into baked 9-inch pie shell and bake at 325° for 30 minutes. When cool top with whipped cream to which you have added 2 drops almond extract. Pie is rich and sweet, so I prefer not to sweeten whipped cream for it.

Pumpkin Pie

(9-inch pie; 6 cuts)

Try squash in the same recipe.

>1½ cups cooked or canned pumpkin
>1½ cups milk or milk and cream or evaporated milk
>3 eggs
>¾ cup brown or white sugar
>¼ teaspoon salt
>1 teaspoon cinnamon
>1 teaspoon nutmeg
>½ teaspoon ginger

Place your hand on the blender cover before starting the motor. Blend just a few seconds, until smooth, and pour into pastry-lined pie shell. Bake at 450° for 10 minutes, then bake at 350° for 30 minutes longer, or until firm in the center. A piece of outer peel of orange can be blender-grated into the pie. Add with ½ cup milk at the beginning and blend fine before adding other ingredients.

Sour Cream Raisin Pie

(8-inch pie; 5 cuts)

Easiest of raisin pies, and one of the best.

1 cup sour cream
2 eggs
1 cup seeded raisins
¼ teaspoon salt
½ teaspoon nutmeg
1 teaspoon cinnamon
1 teaspoon cornstarch
⅔ cup sugar

Blend a minute or two or until raisins are well chopped. Pour into a baked 8-inch pie shell. Bake at 450° for 10 minutes, then bake at 325° for 25 minutes more. Cool and serve with whipped-cream topping.

6

Dips, Dunks
and Spreads

The chopping, beating and whipping actions of blender blades transform solids into smooth-as-satin mixtures that pile in a bowl to make a cocktail dip, or almost instantly convert them into chopped pieces as fine as you may want for a spread. The blender is your servant: it will swallow up the garlic and the parsley, making them one with the cheese; it will create *pâté de foie gras* for you out of the liver of the Christmas goose; it will transform peanuts, pecans or cashews into nut butter.

In general you'll need about ¼ cup liquid to start your mixing action for dips and spreads. When they should contain chopped ingredients, add these at the last, and don't let the blender convert them into fine particles. Chopped green pepper and onion or chopped nuts can be distributed perfectly in the mix if you add them just a second or two before you turn the motor off.

Use a rubber spatula with thick mixtures to help things along. Work the top of the mixture, but be careful not to get down into the blades with the motor running. You may end with chopped rubber in your dunk, and it really isn't very good. So poke carefully, and shut off the motor to free the blades if they bog down. Sometimes a quick switching on and off will get things started again. At any rate, never use a metal spoon or knife.

THE DIPS AND DUNKS, MOSTLY CHEESE

The cheese bowl is almost a necessity of modern entertaining. Any and all kinds of cheese convert to dips and spreads very neatly. Very soft mixtures go into a bowl, to be surrounded with crackers, potato chips, vegetables like crisp cauliflower florets and carrot sticks, all meant for dipping and dunking.

Heavier mixtures can be piled in a bowl or molded into an attractive shape, and should be accompanied by a butter knife for spreading on the crackers, rye bread or Melba toast.

Have cheese at room temperature. Make your mixture a day ahead, to let the flavors blend and ripen.

Avocado Cream Cheese Dip

(About 1 ½ cups)

Pale-green and pretty.

    2 3-ounce packages cream cheese
    1 fully ripe avocado, cut in pieces
    1 tablespoon lemon juice
      Thin slice of medium-sized onion
    ¼ teaspoon salt
    3 tablespoons cream
      Few drops green coloring

Blend ingredients until smooth, using a rubber spatula to push down the top of the mixture if necessary. If it's slow blending, stop the motor and use the spatula around the blades. The green coloring isn't necessary, but it helps accent the avocado color which otherwise is pretty well paled by the cheese.

Blue Cheese Dip with Sauterne

(1 ½ cups plus)

Gourmet's choice!

    ½ pound blue cheese (or Roquefort, Gorgonzola),
        broken up
      3-ounce package cream cheese
    ¼ cup sauterne
    1 teaspoon Worcestershire
      Sliver garlic
    3 or 4 sprigs parsley

Blend until smooth, using rubber spatula as necessary. You could make this with beer instead of sauterne. That's good, too—and *different!*

Brie or Camembert with Bacon

(Almost a pint)

One of my favorites.

Cook until crisp, then break into blender
> ½ pound bacon

Add
> ¼ cup cream
> ½ pound cream cheese
> Thin slice from small onion
> 3 sections Brie or Camembert
> 1 tablespoon lemon juice
> Dash cayenne pepper

Blend until smooth. This has a satiny texture and **wonderful** flavor. Use fully ripened Brie or Camembert (soft).

Clam and Cheese Dip

(Around 1 ½ cups)

A real palate pleaser.

> 7-ounce can clams with ¼ cup of their **liquor**
> 2 3-ounce packages cream cheese
> 2 teaspoons cut chives or green-onion tops
> ¼ teaspoon salt
> 1 teaspoon Worcestershire
> 3 drops tabasco sauce
> 1 tablespoon lemon juice
> 4 or 5 sprigs parsley

Blend until smooth, using spatula as **necessary.**

Cottage Cheese Dip

(About 1 ½ cups)

Thin it for a delicious dressing for salad.

> 1 cup cottage cheese
> ¼ pound blue cheese, crumbled

1 thin slice medium-sized onion
    Dash each: Worcestershire, tabasco
    Tiny sliver garlic
¼ cup sour cream

Beat until very smooth. Everybody, just everybody, likes this one!

Tri-Cheese Spread with Almonds

(About 2 cups)

Crunchy, this one!

1 cup crumbled blue cheese
1 cup diced process Swiss
½ cup diced sharp process Cheddar
1 tablespoon Worcestershire
1 cup sour cream
1 sliver garlic
2 teaspoons paprika

Blend everything until very smooth, then add and blend until chopped

½ cup salted almonds

Two-Cheese Spread with Horse-radish

(About 1 ½ cups)

Unusual, and unusually good!

½ pound cottage cheese
1 3-ounce package cream cheese
1 tablespoon fresh-grated horse-radish
½ teaspoon paprika
½ teaspoon dry mustard
    About 5 or 6 sprigs parsley
½ teaspoon poultry seasoning
½ teaspoon salt

Blend thoroughly and serve as a dunk. Nobody'll be able to guess what the seasoning is.

Cottage Cheese and Shrimp Dip

(1 ¾ cups)

Good on celery.

½ pound fresh cooked shrimps or 5-ounce can
8 ounces cream cheese
3 tablespoons chili sauce
5 or 6 blades of chives, cut
1 tablespoon lemon juice
   Dash Worcestershire
¼ cup cream or milk
½ teaspoon salt

Blend to very smooth mixture, using rubber spatula as necessary.

Cream Cheese and Cheddar Spread

(About 2 cups)

One of the best.

¼ cup cream
¼ cup piccalilli
½ teaspoon salt
½ teaspoon celery salt
1 slice medium-sized onion
1 teaspoon Worcestershire
   Dash tabasco
½ pound cream cheese
½ pound Cheddar, cut in cubes

Whip mixture in the blender until very smooth and creamy, stirring down with rubber spatula occasionally. The success of this spread depends largely on the Cheddar—use the sharpest you can find. Smoked Cheddar is good.

Deviled Ham and Cheese Spread with Sherry

(About 1 ½ cups)

Piquant, this!

½ pound cream cheese
1 3-ounce can deviled ham

¼ cup sherry
2 tablespoons drained sweet-pickle relish
1 slice medium-sized onion
1 teaspoon Worcestershire
¼ teaspoon dry mustard
¼ teaspoon salt
Dash garlic powder or thin sliver garlic

Blend ingredients until very smooth, using spatula as necessary.

Green Dunk (Water Cress)

(Around 2 cups)

Very attractive to the eye as well as to the palate.

½ pound cream cheese
1 slice small onion
Sliver garlic
1 bunch water cress, washed and dried
3 tablespoons lemon juice
½ teaspoon salt
¼ teaspoon white pepper
1 tablespoon horse-radish

Blend until smooth, using spatula now and then at the start. Thin this with sour cream or mayonnaise for a fish sauce or salad dressing. My family loves it on shredded cabbage.

Liptauer Cheese

(Over 2 cups)

A continental specialty for your nicest parties.

1 pound cream cheese, broken up
½ cup sour cream
¼ pound softened butter
1 tablespoon anchovy paste
2 teaspoons capers
2 shallots or 1 small onion, quartered
½ teaspoon salt
1 tablespoon paprika
2 teaspoons caraway seeds

Whip to a smooth blend. Mold this mixture in a bowl if you like. It is irresistibly, tantalizingly good.

Pink Dunk
(About 1 ½ cups)

Shocking pink and startling, but very good!

½ pound cream cheese
6 cooked or canned baby beets
1 tablespoon tarragon vinegar
2 tablespoons lemon juice
¼ teaspoon celery salt
½ teaspoon salt
1 slice medium-sized onion
Dash tabasco

Blend until smooth and thick. You have to reassure people about this one, for they invariably draw back at first sight of the very pinkness of it, thinking you must have got into the Easter-egg coloring. Tell them quickly it's beets; they'll keep coming back for more! Horse-radish is a good addition. Pickled beets can be used, then you can skip the vinegar and lemon juice.

Port and Cheddar
(1 cup)

Use the sharpest of Cheddar; this is good!

¼ cup port wine (or sherry)
2 tablespoons cream
¼ teaspoon paprika
Dash onion salt
½ pound very sharp Cheddar, diced

Blend until smooth. This one is nice molded in a small bowl. Maybe you'd better double the recipe.

Sardine and Cheese Spread
(About 1 ½ cups)

Two cheeses, one fish.

1 can boneless, skinless sardines

  ¼ pound Roquefort or blue cheese
  6 ounces (2 small packages) cream cheese
  ¼ cup diced green pepper
  1 tablespoon chives (or 6 long stems, cut)
  1 teaspoon prepared mustard

Use the oil from the sardines as well as the fish. Blend everything until very smooth and creamy, using your spatula at first.

Savory Cheese

(About 1 ½ cups)

A very popular type.

  2 tablespoons cream
  1 tablespoon melted butter
  ¼ pound Roquefort-type cheese
  1 3-ounce package cream cheese
  1 tablespoon Worcestershire
  ¼ teaspoon salt
  ½ teaspoon paprika
  ¼ green pepper, in pieces
  2 dozen stuffed olives

Blend everything until creamy. You could use olive liquid instead of the cream for a little more pungency—not that you need it!

Tomato Cheese Spread

(Over a cupful)

With fresh tomatoes.

  1 sliver garlic
  2 ripe tomatoes, cut in pieces
  ½ pound cream cheese
  1 teaspoon Worcestershire
  ½ teaspoon salt
  Thin slice of a small onion

Blend until smooth.

Tomato Dunk

(About 1 ⅔ cups)

Good without, better with, fish.

½ pound cream cheese
1 dill pickle, cut in pieces
2 tablespoons pickle juice
1 can tomato paste
1 slice small onion
3 anchovy fillets or smoked oysters or mussels
    (optional)

Blend ingredients until smooth, using spatula as needed. Mold this one. You could use tomato sauce instead of tomato paste for blander seasoning.

SOME NON-CHEESE DIPS AND SPREADS

Avocado Dip

(Will please 4 of you)

Doubles as salad dressing.

1 soft ripe avocado, peeled and cut in pieces
1 slice onion
3 tablespoons mayonnaise
    Juice ½ lemon
    About ½ teaspoon salt
3 drops tabasco sauce

Blend smooth and let ripen in the refrigerator for an hour.

Guacamole

(About 1 ½ cups)

Pronounce it hwoc-a-MO-lay.

1 ripe tomato, cut in pieces
2 soft avocados
1 green onion, in pieces

1 teaspoon salt
Fresh-ground black pepper
3 tablespoons lemon juice
2 canned green chili peppers

Blend until smooth. Serve as a dip, or pile on sliced tomatoes for an appetizer. If you'd rather have it blander than the Mexicans like their specialty, skip the chili peppers.

Deviled Ham Dip

(Double this amount for more than 6)

Good in sandwiches, too.

2 3-ounce cans deviled ham
2 hard-cooked eggs, in pieces
1 teaspoon horse-radish
2 tablespoons diced pickle (or thereabouts)
1 tablespoon milk

Blend smooth and serve with corn chips, for a change.

Pâté de Foie Gras (or a Reasonable Facsimile)

(About 1 ½ cups)

This foie is not so gras, being from chicken, not goose.

Sauté
½ pound chicken livers in
¼ pound butter with
1 slice onion

Place in blender with
¼ pound fresh mushrooms, raw
¼ cup sherry wine
1 teaspoon salt
Dash pepper

Blend everything together until smooth. Pack in a mold and chill. You can use calf's liver either sautéed or simmered, plus melted butter and the other ingredients. That's good, too. Ps-st! You can steal some of the baby's canned chopped liver for a paste like this. Makes it even easier.

Tomato Sour Cream Dip

(Over a cupful)

Coral colored.

½ cup tomato sauce
½ cup thick sour cream **(dairy kind)**
½ teaspoon salt
  Dash black pepper
 1 slice onion
¼ cup prepared horse-radish

Blend until smooth. You could add a few strips of parsley. This is a good sauce for cold meat as well as a dip for chips and vegetables.

SPREADS FOR BREADS

There are thousands of these that you can make beautifully in a blender, I'm sure, and many combinations will occur to you after you've tried a few. The blender grinds nuts, chops carrots, minces ham for spreads. Work with small amounts, and use the rubber spatula as you need to, with the motor off, so that you can get down into the blades.

All of the preceding dips and dunks qualify as sandwich spreads, too.

Almond, Cheese and Marmalade Spread

(More than a cupful)

Ladies' choice.

 1 3-ounce package cream cheese, cut in pieces
½ cup orange marmalade
¼ cup salted almonds

Have cheese at room temperature. Blend until almonds are chopped fairly fine. If you need liquid to help things along, make it orange juice. This one is nice for rolled tea-party sandwiches.

Apricot Nut Spread

(About 1 cup)

For dainty sandwiches.

1 cup well-drained soaked dried apricots
¼ cup walnuts
¼ cup mayonnaise

Blend, leaving nuts chopped, not minced. You can use the big, soft apricots without soaking. They needn't be completely softened.

Banana, Prune and Peanut Spread

(1 cup, plus)

Kiddies' choice!

1 banana, in pieces
½ cup drained prunes, packed in cup
½ cup salted peanuts

Blend until nuts are quite fine. You can add mayonnaise if you like or a tablespoon of lemon juice. Good on whole wheat for the kids.

Bean Spread

(Around a cupful)

Lunch-box special.

1 cup baked beans, canned or your own
1 pickle, dill or other, cut up
2 tablespoons mayonnaise

Blend until pickle is nicely chopped. You could add catsup. Good sandwiched with crisp bacon strips.

Carrot Sandwich Spread

(Makes 4 sandwiches)

A general favorite.

2 large carrots, cut in pieces

½ cup salted peanuts
¼ cup mayonnaise

Blend until carrots and peanuts are chopped medium fine.
Coarse-cut cabbage and some diced celery can be added with a
little more dressing to make a crunchy variation.

Chicken Salad Spread

(1 ¼ cups)

Canned chicken makes it easy.

5½-ounce jar boned chicken, broken up
1 pimiento
¼ green pepper, diced
1 small stalk celery, diced
½ teaspoon salt
About ¼ cup mayonnaise

Blend to smooth mixture, not too fine.

Chicken or Turkey Salad Spread

(Enough for 6 sandwiches)

Best when broiled.

1 cup diced chicken or turkey
1 cup diced celery
1 tablespoon sweet-pickle relish or 1 small pickle
⅓ cup mayonnaise or other dressing
Salt, pepper

Blend until finely chopped, using rubber spatula for even mincing with motor off, of course. For something delicious spread
this on split buns, top with cheese and broil.

Dried Beef Spread

(About 1 ½ cups)

Good on whole wheat.

2 ounces dried beef
½ cup diced Cheddar cheese

    ¾ cup salted peanuts
    1 hard-cooked egg, quartered
    1 pimiento
    ½ cup mayonnaise or cooked dressing
Blend until well mixed and as fine as you like it.

Dried Beef and Tomato Spread

(For 6 hot sandwiches)

This can be your lunch.

    4 ounces dried beef
    1 cup diced sharp cheese
    1 can condensed tomato soup
    1 slice onion
Blend smooth, then either top your bread and broil until hot or heat first and spoon over toasted bread. This is even good cold

Egg and Cheese Spread

(More than a cupful)

A sandwich and soup equals lunch.

    ¼ pound process pimiento cheese, diced
    4 hard-cooked eggs, quartered
    2 tablespoons cream
    ½ cup mayonnaise
    1 slice green pepper
      Salt, pepper
Blend until well mixed, but leave green pepper in discernible pieces.

Fig Spread

(For 4 sandwiches)

Try this on the young ones, after school.

   10 dried figs, soaked 5 minutes in hot water, cut up,
      stems removed
    ¼ cup salted peanuts

¼ cup peanut butter
¼ cup maple sirup

Blend until well mixed. Good on Boston brown bread. If the peanuts have skins, O.K. Don't bother to remove them.

Fruit Nut Spread

(For 6 sandwiches)

Teatime treat.

1 apple, cored, in pieces
1 cup raisins
1 cup walnuts
½ cup orange juice
1 tablespoon lemon juice
Dash salt

Blend until mixture is a spreadable paste.

Garden Fresh Spread

(A little over a cupful)

Nice on fresh white bread.

¼ cup Basic French Dressing (page 192)
¼ pound sharp cheese, cubed
½ cucumber, in pieces
1 carrot, sliced
Salt to taste

Blend until carrots are in fairly fine pieces. A few cubes of crisp cabbage or some cauliflower florets may be added.

Ham Spread

(1 cup)

A real quickie.

2 small tins deviled ham
1 slice onion
1 slice green pepper
¼ cup mayonnaise

Blend until smooth. You could add a pickle.

Maple Honey Butter
(1 ½ cups)

A spread or a sauce.

½ cup honey
½ cup maple sirup
½ cup softened butter

Blend until smooth. This could double as a sauce for pudding or ice cream if you'd cut down the butter or even omit it entirely. And, of course, it's easy to make maple-honey *nut* butter by adding pecans.

Meat Spread
(About 1 cup)

Helps use leftovers.

1 cup sliced roast meat (beef, veal, pork or lamb), cut in squares
1 slice onion
¼ cup mayonnaise
1 teaspoon prepared horse-radish
¼ cup cut celery
½ teaspoon salt

Blend ingredients until meat is finely minced, using spatula as necessary after stopping motor.

Nut Butter
(About a cupful)

So easy and so good.

1 cup salted peanuts, pecans, almonds or cashews
2 tablespoons salad oil or melted butter (optional)

You can make Nut Butter without salad oil, as nuts furnish their own oil, but it takes longer, requires a lot of stopping and starting of the motor and use of the rubber spatula. If the nuts aren't salted, add salt to suit yourself. You may stop blending when the nuts are very fine, but not quite a paste, if you like, and you may use them that way for casserole toppings, curry accompaniments, dressing for cooked vegetables. Ever taste pecan butter? It's delicious and then some!

Olive, Cheese and Bacon Spread

(For 6 sandwiches)

This is one you'll enjoy.

1 cup stuffed olives
¼ pound process cheese, any kind, cubed
4 strips bacon, cooked crisp

Blend ingredients to smooth spread. Add cream or liquid from olives to facilitate things if mixture is too thick to move.

Orange, Cheese and Pecan Filling

(1 ¼ cups)

Fine for a wedding reception.

1 cup pecans
¼ cup orange juice
   Outer peel of ½ orange, in strips
2 3-ounce packages cream cheese

Blend until well mixed and of fairly fine texture.

Salmon and Ripe Olive Spread

(Enough for 6 sandwiches)

Substantial eating.

½ cup salmon
1 small carrot, in pieces
¼ cup chopped ripe olives (You can buy them that
   way.)
¼ cup diced celery
¼ cup mayonnaise
1 teaspoon lemon juice
   Salt

Blend until vegetables are finely chopped; stop motor often and stir down contents. Tip: a stalk of celery is almost as good a spatula as a spatula, and you could even use it with the motor running!

Sardine Spread

(About ¾ cup)

Try this on Melba toast.

    1 small tin sardines in mustard or tomato sauce
    1 tablespoon lemon juice
    1 hard-cooked egg, quartered
    2 tablespoons mayonnaise

Blend to smooth paste.

Shrimp or Lobster Paste

(1 cup)

An excellent canapé cover.

    1 small can shrimps (4½ or 5 ounces) or 1 cup cooked
       shrimps or lobster meat
    2 tablespoons lemon juice or tarragon vinegar
       Salt, onion salt, celery salt
    2 tablespoons chili sauce
    2 tablespoons mayonnaise

Blend to a fine paste. Capers are also good with the spread if you have them. A teaspoonful is enough.

Walnut, Green Pepper and Cheese Spread

(Well over a cup)

This can be molded for a party.

    1 green pepper, diced
    ½ cup walnuts
    ½ pound cream cheese, diced
    ¼ cup cream
       Salt, pepper
       Dash Worcestershire

Blend, leaving pepper and nuts in fine pieces.

Water Cress Butter

(Around a cupful)

Full of vitamins!

½ bunch water cress, washed and dried
½ cup soft butter
1 tablespoon lemon juice
½ teaspoon prepared mustard
Salt

Blend until cress is very fine.

7

Drinks

Drinks are what blenders were invented for. The Frozen Daiquiri that comes out of the container the consistency of a sherbet, the thick foamy Chocolate Malted Milk, the Mocha Mint Cooler with its fresh mint blended right in are beverages you can prepare in no other way. How else can you make a drink of pineapple juice and *liquid* carrot?

The drinks you can make in your blender number thousands. Fruits and fruit juices, milk and eggs, even vegetables, can be made into countless wonderful drinkables. The recipes here will get you off to the right start in creating your own combinations. They are all tried and tested. I know you'll enjoy using them.

Cocktails and Drinks Made with Liquor and Wine

This group of recipes represents most of the blender-made favorites in homes and at famous bars. There are a good many "ladies drinks" among them—so called because they are pretty and delicious from the first sip—since the blender is perfect for mixing any drink that's frothy, fluffy or fruited. You'll miss the manhattans and martinis, perhaps. These are cocktails that should be clear, and a blender would make them cloudy. Use your blender for the dozens of drinks that were never meant to be clear!

You can make any drink better in a blender if it's a drink that needs shaking or vigorous mixing. If the recipe says "Shake with ice," give it a whirl in the blender, and it will be better than you've ever had it.

What Do You Need for a Home Bar?

You'll do nicely with the following items, and you could get along very well with less.

Bottled Goods

(1 bottle each)

Light Rum (Better have 2; there are many delightful
   rum drinks!)
Gin
Brandy
Dry Vermouth
Sweet Vermouth
Bourbon
Scotch
Sherry
Crème de Menthe
Grenadine Sirup
Angostura Bitters
Carbonated Water (½ dozen bottles)

Bar Utensils and Accessories

Blender (of course!)
Ice Crusher
Strainer
Jigger, measuring 1½ ounces on one side, ¾ ounce on
   the other
Long Mixing Spoon
Mixing Glass (for the martinis not in this book!)
Set of standard Measuring Spoons
Glass Measuring Cup, marked in ounces
Bottle Opener
Corkscrew
Some kind of Juicer
Straws for the drinks to be sipped
Glasses
Stuffed Olives, Pickled Onions, Cherries

There's no need to buy a lot of glassware. Use what you have.
Sherbet glasses will do nicely for the frozen drinks. These are
the three sizes used most often: 5-ounce cocktail glass to hold
3-ounce drink; 8-ounce highball glass; wine glass or claret cup.

Tall lemonade glasses (12 ounce) are nice for the collinses. Old Fashioned glasses (6 ounce) are useful, too, but certainly no necessity.

How Long Do You Blend a Drink?

Only a few seconds for most drinks. Just on, off and pour. Drinks of the daiquiri type which you want frozen or semifrozen may take a minute. You'll rapidly catch on to how long it takes in the kind of machine you have.

How Much Ice Do You Use?

A rule of thumb: about ½ cup cracked ice per drink; twice as much if you want it frozen. When you make as many as 4 drinks at once you don't need ½ cup ice for each; 1 cup usually is enough for four. The amount of ice is really a matter of personal preference. A lot dilutes your drink, but maybe you want it diluted!

Always crack or crush ice before putting it into the blender. Ice cubes may damage the cutting edges of the blender blades. Use an ice crusher (a good wall-type ice crusher costs 8 or 9 dollars), or a canvas bag and mallet or hammer. Another technique suggested by one blender manufacturer is to drive an ice pick or nail into the center of each ice cube while still in the tray, to crack them. The blender readily transforms cracked ice into shaved ice.

Bartender's Ballad: "An extra chill is an extra thrill."

Fill your glasses with cracked ice while they wait to be filled. Chill your blender container and ingredients.

Table of Equivalents

1 jigger = 1½ ounces, or 3 tablespoons
1 pony = 1 ounce, or 2 tablespoons
  juice of 1 lemon = about 3 tablespoons
  juice of 1 lime = about 1½ tablespoons
  dash = about ⅛ teaspoon
4 ounces = ½ cup or 8 tablespoons

SUGAR in blender drinks. While very finely granulated sugar, known as bar or powdered (not confectioners') sugar, is required for most drinks, it is not necessary when you use a blender. You get perfect solution whether you use granulated, bar sugar or a sirup. Rule of thumb about sugar and lemon: 1 jigger of lemon juice calls for 1 teaspoon of sugar to sweeten.

THE ALEXANDER FAMILY

Alexanders are after-dinner drinks. Never serve them before a meal. They're too rich and sweet. Chill the ingredients first if you have time.

Alexander

(4 drinks)

Tastes so good!

4 ounces gin
4 ounces whipping cream
4 ounces *crème de cacao*
About 1 cup cracked ice

Switch motor on for just a few seconds, then off. **Strain.**

Brandy Alexander

Substitute brandy for gin.

Alexander's Southern Cousin

Substitute Southern Comfort for gin. This one's **perfection!**

Alexander's Sister

(4 drinks)

See the resemblance?

4 ounces gin
4 ounces whipping cream
4 ounces crème de menthe
About 1 cup cracked ice

Blend for a few seconds and strain out ice.

Pump Room Alexander

(4 drinks)

Gets a fourth partner!

    3 ounces gin (or brandy)
    3 ounces whipping cream
    3 ounces *crème de cacao*
    3 ounces crème de menthe
    1 cup or more cracked ice
Blend a few seconds; strain out ice.

Bud's Special

(2 drinks)

A shirttail relative.

    4 ounces Cointreau
    2 ounces heavy cream
    Dash of angostura bitters
    About 1 cup cracked ice
Switch on the motor for about 6 seconds; then off, and strain.

Grasshopper

(4 drinks)

An attractive, popular relative.

    4 ounces white *crème de cacao*
    4 ounces green crème de menthe
    4 ounces whipping cream
    About 1 cup cracked ice
Switch on motor for a few seconds; then off, and strain. Brown *crème de cacao* was originally used in this drink, and still is in some cocktail bars.

Pink Elephant

Strangely, this is a Grasshopper made with pink crème de menthe! White *crème de cacao* is a must in this case.

The 5:15 Cocktail

(4 drinks)

Or do you catch the 5:45?

    4 ounces curaçao
    4 ounces French vermouth
    4 ounces whipping cream
    1 cup or more cracked ice

On again, off again, strain again. Then there's another Alexander brother known as Whizdoodle, composed of equal parts Scotch, gin, cream and *crème de cacao*. But let's get on to something else!

THE COLLINSES

These are the tall refreshers, the lemonades with a concealed kick. They're for the hot days of summer and sipping through straws. Put ice cubes in your tallest glasses for them.

Tom Collins

(1 drink)

Most gregarious of the Collins boys!

    1 jigger lemon juice (lime is good, too)
    1 jigger gin
    1 teaspoon sugar
    ½ cup cracked ice

Give these ingredients a quick whirl in your blender, and pour over 2 or 3 ice cubes in a tall glass (10 or 12 ounce). Add a cherry, and fill glass with seltzer. A mint-leaf garnish is pretty.

John Collins

Same thing, only with whisky instead of gin.

Rum or Brandy Collins

Same pattern, different liquor.

Apricot Collins

(1 drink)

Slightly different, wholly delightful.

Juice ½ lemon
½ teaspoon grenadine
2 ounces apricot brandy or liqueur
1 cup cracked ice

Blend 30 seconds. Pour over a couple of ice cubes and fill glass with sparkling water. Try this with any of the fruit brandies.

Mint Collins, Pump Room

(1 drink)

Mint Collins is also known as Irish Rose.

1 jigger gin
1 jigger lemon juice
1 jigger green crème de menthe
¼ teaspoon sugar
½ cup cracked ice

Give it a whirl and strain into 10-ounce glass. Add an ice cube, fill with seltzer and decorate with fruit.

Mint Collins with Fresh Mint

Put 2 or 3 mint leaves into the blender with your other collins ingredients. Best with Tom, John and rum collinses.

DAIQUIRIS

Most people like daiquiris to be of a slushy consistency—which takes 5 to 8 ounces cracked ice for one—but with more ice it is possible to serve them really sherbeted. Use sherbet glasses, if you haven't big champagne glasses, and short straws.

If you don't want your daiquiri frozen, don't blend it more than just a few seconds.

Chill the blender and the rum.

Frozen Daiquiri

(1 drink)

World famous, and no wonder.

1 jigger light rum
Juice ½ lime (1 if small and not very juicy)
1 teaspoon sugar
5 ounces ice (more for sherbet consistency)

Blend ingredients until you have the texture you want. If you use 10 ounces or so of ice, you may find you have to use a barspoon or spatula to scrape the frozen mixture back into the blades. Be sure to stop the motor first!

Banana Daiquiri

Some people like this! Put half a banana per daiquiri into the blender.

Mint Daiquiri

You couldn't make this one without a blender, and it's delightful. Just put a couple of fresh mint leaves into the blender with each daiquiri.

Frozen Peach Daiquiri

(Makes 6)

Some drinks are merely wonderful, but some are oo-oo wonderful! This one's oooo!

1 cup Bacardi rum
Juice of 3 limes
1 box (12 ounces) frozen peaches
1 pint crushed ice

Blend this mixture (break up peaches slightly first) a minute or so, until it is nice and slushy. This could be your dessert! An utterly luxurious touch may be achieved by adding a jigger of Grand Marnier to this lovely concoction.

Strawberry Daiquiri

Same idea, but with a package of frozen strawberries instead of peaches. You could use fresh fruit, too, of course.

OTHER FRUITED DAIQUIRIS

Fresh or canned pineapple makes an elegant one. Apricots, cherries, even melon may be used. Follow the standard of a jigger of rum and the juice of ½ lime per person. If the fruit is sweetened, don't add more sugar.

Bacardi Cocktail

(2 drinks)

Daiquiri with grenadine, a pretty pink.

    2 jiggers Bacardi rum
      Juice of 2 limes
    1 jigger grenadine
    1 cup (or more) cracked ice

Blend it short to sip from the glass; longer and with more ice to frappé it and drink with straws.

Cuban Special

(For 2)

Really delightful!

    2 jiggers Bacardi rum
      Juice 1 lime
    2 jiggers fresh pineapple juice
    2 teaspoons apricot brandy
    1 cup (or more) cracked ice

Blend 1 minute or more, to the consistency you like. To get fresh pineapple juice, all you have to do is blend cut-up fresh pineapple!

Frosted Pineapple

(For 2)

Almost a daiquiri, and one of the most delectable drinks ever invented!

2 jiggers light rum
3 slices fresh pineapple, pared, cored, cut up
1 tablespoon sugar
1 pint cracked ice

Blend to a slushy consistency. Garnish with mint, or blend with two sprigs of mint. Leave out the rum and it's still good!

Scarlet O'Hara

(4 drinks)

She's kin to a Bacardi.

6 ounces Southern Comfort
½ cup cranberry juice (or cranberry sauce)
Juice 1 lime
1 cup cracked ice

Blend a few seconds, leave ice in, and if you like fill glasses half full of cracked ice before adding drink. Originally this drink had a quarter of a peach in the bottom of each glass. Cranberry Cocktail, cranberry sauce of the homemade kind or the canned sauce may be used.

THE MILKY WAY—A collection of drinks made with milk, eggs and liquors

When you use a recipe calling for 1 egg or 1 egg white for 1 drink, you don't always use 2 eggs or 2 whites for 2 drinks. In most cases 1 egg will do for 2 drinks as well as for one.

Don't prolong the blending of a drink containing milk or egg or you'll get too much foam. Some foam is very nice, but nobody wants to acquire a white mustache drinking through the bubbles.

Eggnog

(1 drink)

New Year's cheer, but good any time.

1 jigger rum, brandy, whisky or sherry
5 ounces milk or milk and cream
1 egg
1 teaspoon sugar
2 ice cubes, cracked

Blend just a few seconds, strain into glass and top with nutmeg. One of the best of all eggnogs is the preceding, made with ½ rum, ½ brandy.

Hot Eggnog

For whed your doze is stobbed ub—or for any cold day.

Use the preceding recipe. Rinse out the blender container with hot water, put in egg and give it a quick whirl. Then gradually add combination of milk, sugar and liquor heated just to the boiling point, no further. Blend about 2 seconds and serve at once in preheated mugs.

Hot Rum Cow

(2 servings in mugs)

Delicious and not too rich.

2 ounces light rum
2 teaspoons sugar
¼ teaspoon vanilla
10 ounces milk

Heat ingredients but don't let them boil. Pour into blender, which has been rinsed with hot water, switch on the motor for just a few seconds and pour into heated mugs or cups. Add nutmeg. Be sure to put your hand lightly on the blender cover when you start the motor for this, or it will splash. Incidentally, this is good cold, too.

Hot Rum and Brandy Punch

(1 drink)

Dark rum, for a change.

½ jigger Jamaica rum
½ jigger brandy
1 teaspoon sugar
1 cup hot milk
  Dash of bitters or sprinkle of nutmeg
Heat ingredients, turn into warmed blender, blend a few seconds and serve in a hot mug. This is good cold, too. Omit the bitters and add cracked ice. Blend and strain or not as you like. Slight ice dilution is pleasant.

Banana Cow

(1 tall glass or 2 small ones)

This one's good. Skip the rum and you can give it to the kiddies.

1 ripe banana, cut in pieces
1 tablespoon sugar
3 ounces milk
1 jigger light rum
1 cup cracked ice
Blend a few seconds to liquefy the banana before you add ice. Then give it another quick whirl and strain out the ice.

And then there are those morning cocktails that are supposed to fix everything. This one's from Chicago's Ambassador East Hotel and is called

The Morning's Morning

(1 drink)

First drink of the day.

1½ ounces cognac
¾ ounce *crème de cacao*

    ¾ ounce Jamaica rum
    1 egg
    1 teaspoon sugar
    5 ounces milk
    Cracked ice

Blend until well mixed but not too frothy, and strain out ice.
This goes into a 12-ounce glass and gets a topping of nutmeg. If
you make 2 at once, use 2 eggs. One won't do for 2 drinks as in
most other cocktails.

Sunday Morning Cocktail

(For 1)

Coffee, no milk, in this.

    1 jigger cognac
    ½ jigger strong black coffee
    ½ jigger port
    1 egg
    ½ teaspoon sugar
    ½ cup cracked ice

Run blender about 10 seconds; strain.

And—Oh Goody!—Ice Cream!

You can use vanilla ice cream instead of whipping cream in
any drink like the Alexander, or try one of these bright ideas.

Crème de Café

(Fills 8 champagne glasses)

A man's drink, and slightly sensational!

    1 cup bourbon
    1 cup triple-strength cold black coffee
    1 pint vanilla ice cream

Just on and off with the blender switch. No ice; use frozen coffee
if you like: 3 teaspoons with 1 cup ice water.

Cricket

(For 2)

Reminds you of an Alexander.

2 jiggers *crème de cacao*
1 jigger brandy
1 scoop vanilla ice cream
Switch on, switch off.

Golden Gate

(For 2)

Not bad!

2 jiggers gin or light rum
½ pint orange ice or sherbet
Blend smooth.

White Cargo

Same as Golden Gate, only with vanilla ice cream. Some of the boys use ½ pint gin or rum and ½ pint ice cream for this, but that's pretty potent!

Fizzes, Flips and Eggish Drinks

Remember, don't overblend, or you'll be burying your nose in bubbles to get to the drink!

Bacardi Flip (Rum Flip)

(4 drinks)

This one's good 2 ways.

3 eggs
4 jiggers Bacardi rum
4 teaspoons sugar
Dash angostura bitters
1 cup cracked ice

Blend just a few seconds; strain. Add a twist of outer rind of lemon to each serving. Or you may skip the bitters and lemon and sprinkle the drink with nutmeg.

Cherry Flip

(2 drinks)

Delicious!

   1 egg
   6 ounces Danish cherry wine
   2 teaspoons sugar
   1 tablespoon lemon juice
   ½ cup cracked ice
Blend and leave the ice in.

Claret Flip

(For 2)

Dusty pink, and very nice.

   1 egg
   6 ounces claret, Burgundy or cabernet
   1 tablespoon sugar
   ½ cup cracked ice
Blend about 10 seconds and leave ice in. Sprinkle with nutmeg or add a dash of bitters.

Port or Sherry Flip

Same thing, only with the sweeter wine you can cut the sugar down to a teaspoonful for 2 drinks, or skip it altogether.

Clover Club

(For 2)

Frequent feminine choice.

   2 jiggers gin
   1 jigger grenadine
   3 tablespoons lemon or lime juice

       1 egg white
       1 cup cracked ice
Blend a few seconds; strain or not. For a less sweet drink cut
down the grenadine slightly.

Clover Leaf

This is a Clover Club floating a mint leaf, or better, a nice clean
clover leaf from your back yard.

Royal Clover Club

For this variation use the egg yolk instead of the white. You can
use 2 yolks for 2 drinks if you like.

September Morn

Make the Clover Club with rum instead of gin, and if you have it
use raspberry sirup instead of grenadine.

Coffee with Kirsch Cocktail (Café au Kirsch)
(For 2)

Better after dinner.

       2 ounces kirsch (or ½ kirsch, ½ cognac)
       2 ounces strong cold coffee
       1 egg white
    1½ teaspoons sugar
       1 cup cracked ice
Blend a few seconds and strain or not. Use a teaspoon of soluble
coffee and let the ice dilute your drink if you've no pot of coffee
on hand. It's quicker than making coffee and waiting for it to
cool.

Coffee Cocktail
(For 2)

*There's no coffee in it, but it looks and tastes sur-
prisingly coffeeish.*

       2 ounces port

2 ounces rum or brandy
1 egg
1 teaspoon sugar
1 cup cracked ice

Switch on the motor; switch it off. Strain or not. It's a good morning cocktail.

Foamy Orange Lime Cocktail

(For 5 or 6)

Pleasantly innocuous.

½ cup orange juice
2 tablespoons lime juice
½ cup white port or angelica
1 tablespoon sugar
1 egg white
1 cup cracked ice

Blend a few seconds and serve with ice in the drink.

Grapefruit Fizz

(4 drinks)

Just a little wine.

1 cup grapefruit juice
2 jiggers sherry wine
1 egg white
1 tablespoon sugar
1 cup cracked ice

Blend a few seconds and serve without straining.

Green Elevator (Chartreuse Cocktail)

(2 drinks)

Unusual and most delicious!

2 jiggers green chartreuse
Juice 1 lemon
2 tablespoons grapefruit juice

1 egg white
1 cup cracked ice
Blend a few seconds; strain out ice. Warning: chartreuse is expensive!

Morning Glory
(For 2)

A green flower.

2 jiggers gin
  Juice of 1 lime
1 egg
4 teaspoons green crème de menthe
1 cup cracked ice
Blend a few seconds and strain or not.

Pink Cloud
(4 drinks)

Pinkly pretty!

4 ounces gin
4 ounces pineapple juice
2 ounces grenadine
1 egg white
2 cups cracked ice
Blend in a whirl and leave the ice in.

Pink Lady Number One
(2 drinks)

Such a charming girl!

1 jigger gin
1 tablespoon apple brandy
1 tablespoon lemon juice
1 tablespoon grenadine sirup
1 egg white
½ cup cracked ice
Blend about 10 seconds and leave ice in drink.

Second Pink Lady

(For 2, too)

This one's made with cream, not egg.

2 tablespoons lemon or lime juice
2 tablespoons grenadine sirup
2½ ounces gin
1 jigger heavy cream
½ cup cracked ice

Blend about 15 seconds and leave ice in.

After trying five different drinks, each purporting to be the one and only, the original, the absolute Ramos Gin Fizz, for which New Orleans is famous, I say authentic or not (and I'm told it *really* is!), this one's perfectly delicious.

Ramos Gin Fizz

(For 2)

Justly famous.

1 jigger lemon juice, or ½ lemon, ½ lime juice
1 teaspoon sugar
2 jiggers gin
1 egg white
2 jiggers cream
About 10 drops orange flower water (from drug-store)
½ to 1 cup cracked ice

Blend a few seconds. Some recipes direct you to fill the glass with club soda. We didn't. Advice from a prominent bar manager: "Coat" the glass with the orange flower water. Let it run around inside as you turn the glass, pour out any excess and add your drink. This way you'd probably use more than the 10 drops suggested.

Rum Fizz

(For 2)

Fruited and frothy.

2 jiggers rum
2 ounces lemon juice
2 teaspoons sugar
1 egg or 1 egg white
1 slice canned pineapple, cut up
1 cup cracked ice

Blend a few seconds; leave ice in.

Shamrock Special

(For 2)

Green as the auld sod.

2 jiggers gin
   Juice 2 small limes
2 tablespoons green crème de menthe
1 egg white
1 cup or more cracked ice

Blend long enough to get a sherbety consistency; give it the consistency of a Frozen Daiquiri. You may have to add more ice. If you can find fresh clover leaves, use them for garnish. (The Shamrock cocktail, page 135, is another Irishman.)

Silver Fizz

(Individual drink)

Tall and pale.

1 jigger gin (or use rum if you'd rather)
   Juice ½ lemon
1 teaspoon sugar
1 egg white
½ cup cracked ice

Blend, leaving the ice in. Pour into 8-ounce glass and fill with sparkling water. Nice summer drink, especially as an afternoon pickup.

Golden Fizz and Royal Fizz

These are brothers. Golden Fizz uses the yolk instead of the white. Royal Fizz takes the whole egg.

Sloe Gin Fizz

(For 2)

Known as a girl's first drink; pretty, like pink lemonade.

    Juice 1 lemon
    2 teaspoons sugar
    2 jiggers sloe gin
    ½ cup cracked ice

Blend a few seconds, pour into 8-ounce glasses and fill with carbonated water.

Gin Fizz

Made the same way, only with gin.

A BOUQUET OF ROSES

Rose Cocktail

(For 2)

No thorns in this rose!

    1 jigger gin
    ½ jigger apricot brandy
    ½ jigger French vermouth
    2 teaspoons grenadine
    1 teaspoon lemon juice
    ½ cup cracked ice

Switch on, switch off and strain.

La Vie en Rose

(For 2)

Such a lovely rose!

½ jigger lemon juice
½ jigger grenadine
1 jigger gin
1 jigger kirsch
½ cup cracked ice

Blend just a second or two and strain.

Jack Rose

(For 2)

How'd that man get in here?

1 ounce lime or lemon juice
2 jiggers applejack brandy
2 tablespoons grenadine sirup
1 egg white (not a necessary ingredient, but makes
  it smoother)
½ cup cracked ice

Switch on, switch off and strain.

Mary Rose

(6 to 8 drinks)

Strong, but sweet!

3 ounces cherry brandy
3 ounces gin
6 ounces port wine
1 to 1½ cups cracked ice

Blend fastlike and strain. Serve with a cherry in each drink.

Rose In June

(1 drink)

But good in January, too.

Juice 1 orange
Juice 2 small limes
1 jigger raspberry sirup
1 jigger gin
½ cup cracked ice
Blend quickly and leave ice in drink.

Rosemary

(4 drinks)

Feminine in name only; a good appetizer.

1 jigger cherry brandy
1 jigger French vermouth
2 jiggers gin
½ cup cracked ice
Blend a second or two and strain. Garnish with a cherry for each.

THE SOURS

These drinks will do nicely as appetizers.

Whisky, Gin, Rum or Brandy Sour

(2 drinks)

A general favorite.

2 teaspoons sugar
1 jigger lemon and lime juice
2 jiggers of the preferred liquor
½ to 1 cup cracked ice
On, off, strain and garnish with cherry and ½ slice orange.

Apple Jack Sour

Make this the same way, but use apply brandy. Sweeten with grenadine and sugar—1 teaspoon each.

Special Sour
(For 2)

The only sweetener is that wonderful liqueur, Grand Marnier.

1 jigger Scotch or bourbon
1 jigger lemon juice
1 jigger Grand Marnier liqueur (or orange curaçao)
½ to 1 cup cracked ice
On, off and strain. Garnish with fruit.

ADDED ATTRACTIONS—Some famous cocktails and a few exotic beverages

All-American Cocktail
(For 2)

A pleasant wine drink.

4 ounces Burgundy or claret
1 ounce lemon juice
1 tablespoon sugar
1 cup cracked ice
Blend for just a few seconds and strain, or blend until ice has dissolved.

Bee Bite Cocktail
(2 drinks)

A winsome bee—this doesn't hurt at all!

2 jiggers light rum
  Juice of 2 limes
1 jigger orange juice
2 teaspoons grenadine
1 cup cracked ice

You can run the blender a little longer on this. Don't strain. Use twice as much ice and turn it into a frappéed drink if you like. The Bee Bite, at least this one, is really a Bacardi with orange juice, so perhaps I should have placed it among the daiquiris.

Between the Sheets
(2 drinks)

Good before or after dinner, or as a pick-me-up.

   1 jigger gin or light rum
   1 jigger brandy
   1 jigger Cointreau
   1 jigger lemon juice
   1 cup cracked ice

Switch on the motor, count to 6, switch it off and strain out the ice if any.

Bronx Cocktail
(For 2)

Excellent before-dinner drink.

   1 jigger orange juice
   1 jigger dry vermouth
   1 jigger sweet vermouth
   1 jigger gin
   1 cup cracked ice

Turn the switch, say "I'll have a Bronx, please," turn off the blender and strain or not.

Champêche
(For 2)

To toast a bride!

   1 fresh peach, cut in pieces
   10 ounces ice-cold champagne

Whirl peach to a liquid in blender, stir in champagne and pour into 2 of your best crystal goblets. Some cracked ice in the drink is advisable.

Cherry Blossom

(For 2)

Like pink lemonade!

2 jiggers sloe gin
1 ounce orange juice
1 tablespoon lemon juice
1 tablespoon maraschino cherry juice or
    cherry liqueur
1 cup cracked ice

Blend a few seconds and strain or leave ice in. This is pretty and can be frappéed if you'll double the ice and blend longer.

Cherry Ripe

(2 drinks)

Innocent looking, but——!

2 jiggers gin
1 jigger kirsch
1 jigger cherry brandy
2 cups cracked ice

Blend a minute or long enough to make the mixture sherbety in texture. Pile high in big cocktail glasses and poke a cherry into the top of each. Pour ½ teaspoon cherry brandy around the cherry if you like, but this drink is potent enough anyway!

Cotton Picker Cocktail

(For 2)

A good afternoon pick-me-up.

2 ounces Southern Comfort
2 ounces orange juice
1 ounce rum
1 ounce lemon juice
1 cup cracked ice

Blend, strain or not. More ice will frappé this drink, and that's nice, too. If you frappé it, serve it with straws, of course.

Crème de Menthe Frappé

Convert cracked ice to shaved ice in your blender, pack your glasses with that and pour crème de menthe over the ice to fill the glass. Naturally, use straws. Try this also with *crème de cacao,* curaçao, Grand Marnier or any liqueur that tastes good by itself.

Hawaiian Punch

(2 drinks)

Very exotic, especially if it is served in a coconut.

3 ounces gin or rum
3 ounces coconut milk
1 jigger lemon juice
1 teaspoon curaçao or Grand Marnier
2 teaspoons sugar
  About 2 cups ice

Blend until sherbety. If you want to be *very* fancy, bore a largish hole in one of the coconut eyes, after draining the milk and making the drink, and use a small funnel to put the drink into the coconut from which it can be sipped through straws!

Honolulu Wine Cooler

(4 sizable drinks)

Oh, so refreshing!

1 cup fresh or canned pineapple, cut up
6 ounces any dry white wine
6 ounces sherry
  Juice ½ lemon
1½ cups cracked ice

Blend until pineapple is liquefied, and leave ice in drink. This almost makes the capacity of the blender container, so keep your hand on the blender top when starting the motor—you don't want a splashover!

Marmalade Cocktail

(4 drinks)

Sounds terrible, but it is very nice.

¼ cup marmalade (apricot preserves are good, too)
Juice 2 small lemons
4 jiggers gin
1 cup cracked ice
Blend until smooth.

Millionaire Cocktail

(For 3)

Makes you feel like one!

1 jigger Jamaica rum
1 jigger apricot brandy
1 jigger sloe gin
½ teaspoon grenadine
1 jigger lime juice
1 cup cracked ice
Blend a few seconds and strain or not.

Mint Cocktail

(For 2)

Real mint flavor and a pretty color.

2 sprigs fresh mint
2 jiggers any dry white wine
1½ jiggers gin
½ jigger crème de menthe
½ to 1 cup cracked ice
Blend about 20 seconds. Do not strain.

Opal

(For 2)

Much like an Orange Blossom.

2 jiggers orange juice

 2 jiggers gin
 1 tablespoon Cointreau
   Few drops orange flower water
 ½ cup cracked ice
Blend a few seconds and strain or not.

Orange Blossom

(For 2)

A lovely refresher.

 2 jiggers gin (or rum)
 2 jiggers orange juice
 1 tablespoon lemon juice
 1 teaspoon sugar
 ½ cup (or more) cracked ice
 2 slices orange

Blend all but orange slices for a few seconds, or use more ice and blend to sherbet consistency. Float thin orange slice on drink or hang half orange slice over edge of glass.

Orange Velvet

(4 drinks)

Nice!

 ½ cup California white port
 ½ cup orange juice
 1 tablespoon lemon juice
 1½ cups cracked ice

Blend about 30 seconds. Serve without straining.

Paradise Cocktail

(For 2)

Both pretty and good!

 2 ounces apricot brandy
 2 ounces gin

2 ounces orange juice
½ cup cracked ice
Switch on, switch off. Strain or not.

Pineapple Cooler

(For 2)

There's something about fresh pineapple!

2 jiggers gin
2 slices fresh pineapple, cut in pieces
1 ounce green crème de menthe
1 cup cracked ice
Blend until smooth and leave ice in.

Planter's Punch

(For 2)

A man's drink.

1 jigger orange juice
1 jigger pineapple juice
2 ounces lime or lemon juice
2 teaspoons sugar or grenadine
4 ounces Jamaica rum
1 cup cracked ice
Blend quickly and serve with ice left in and more ice in the glass.
Garnish with fruit—a half slice of orange and a cherry—and add
a sprig of mint.

Poinciana

(For 4)

Richly fruited.

4 jiggers light rum
4 maraschino cherries
2 slices whole orange
2 jiggers apple juice
1 jigger grenadine

Blend 30 seconds or until fruit is liquefied. Strain into glasses half filled with cracked ice.

Presidente

(For 3)

Very Cuban!

2 jiggers Bacardi rum
1 jigger dry vermouth
1 teaspoon grenadine
1 cup cracked ice

Blend just a few seconds, then strain. Garnish with twist of orange peel and a cherry. You can add a teaspoon of orange curaçao if you like.

Red Lion

(4 drinks)

You'll like this.

2 jiggers gin
2 jiggers Grand Marnier
1 jigger orange juice
1 jigger lemon juice
1 cup cracked ice

Blend a few seconds and leave ice in.

Frozen Scotch

(1 drink)

Or bourbon if you'd rather.

1 jigger Scotch
1 jigger lemon juice
1 teaspoon sugar
   About 10 ounces cracked ice

Blend to a sherbet consistency and serve in an Old Fashioned glass if you have it. This is a Pump Room specialty at Chicago's Ambassador East Hotel. It's a good appetizer.

Shamrock

(For 3)

This one's for the men when the women are having Shamrock Special, page 123.

3 jiggers Irish whisky
1 jigger dry vermouth
1 jigger green crème de menthe
1 cup cracked ice

On and off; strain. Add a clover leaf if you have some.

Sidecar

(2 drinks)

Very smooth.

1 jigger lime juice
1 jigger Cointreau or Triple Sec
1 jigger brandy
1 egg white (if you like; not always called for)
½ cup cracked ice

On, off and strain.

Stinger

(For 2)

Very popular after-dinner drink.

1 jigger brandy
1 jigger white crème de menthe
½ cup cracked ice

On, off and strain. There are several special versions of this drink. At the Ambassador East about ½ an egg white would be added for 2 drinks. Stingers also can be nicely served frosted. Increase the ice and blend until you get sherbet consistency. This requires straws, of course.

Wedding Belle

(For 3)

To honor a bride and groom.

1 ounce orange juice
1 ounce cherry brandy
2 ounces gin
2 ounces Dubonnet
1½ cups cracked ice

Blend about 30 seconds and serve with ice in drink. Can be frappéed nicely, too, with longer blending and a little more ice.

Whisper Cocktail

(For 2)

Strictly before dinner!

1 jigger whisky
1 jigger French vermouth
1 jigger Italian vermouth
½ cup cracked ice

Switch on, switch off and strain.

8

More Drinks,

the Nonalcoholic Kind

Your blender will make cabbage or carrot juice for you, liquefy any fruit or vegetable—nuts, coconuts, dates and figs. It will even make drinkable the core of an apple or the shell of an egg. Maybe you want to drink these—I don't. But a blender can make it possible to drink them.

How To Liquefy a Solid in the Blender

Pour water, milk or fruit juice into the blender container until the blades are covered. Add the solid in pieces, a few at a time (for example: 1 carrot, cut up, or 1 apple, in pieces). Cover the container and put your hand lightly on top. Turn the switch and blend first at low speed if your machine has several speeds. Then turn to high speed and run the motor until the food is drinkable. You can add more liquid to thin it if necessary. In general, it takes 2 parts of liquid to 1 of solid to make something you can drink.

Have Ingredients Cold, and Crack the Ice

Drinks made without ice, like the various milk drinks, need to be cold to begin with. Ice should be cracked. Some blender manufacturers let you drop an ice cube or two into a mixture that is to be blended, but as a rule it is much better to use cracked ice, for the sake of protecting the edges of the blender blades and as a precaution against breaking the glass container.

Follow Directions

Read the booklet you got with your blender and follow the manufacturer's directions. Machines vary among themselves, and while they all do the same things, some work faster than others. Timing is a variable factor. One machine may take a little longer to liquefy solids than another.

SIRUPS AS SWEETENERS

It is convenient sometimes to have on hand sirups to use as sweeteners and flavorers of blended drinks. These are the ones you'll use most frequently:

Simple Sirup or Sugar Sirup

> 1 cup sugar
> 1 cup water

Boil sugar and water together for 5 minutes and pour into jar with a cover. Cool and keep in the refrigerator to use as needed.

Caramel Sirup

> *Wonderful for coffee drinks, milk shakes and malteds.*

> 1 cup sugar
> 1 cup water

Put the sugar in a heavy iron skillet and melt, stirring constantly, until it becomes a golden-brown sirup. Add water and keep stirring (mixture will lump when water is added) until sugar becomes a sirup. Store in covered jar. Two tablespoons of this plus a cup of milk equal something delectable.

Chocolate Sirup

> 3 ounces unsweetened chocolate, melted
> 1 cup sugar
> ⅔ cup water

Combine ingredients and stir over low heat until blended and smooth. Keep in a covered jar in the refrigerator.

Cocoa Sirup

1 cup cocoa
¾ cup sugar
½ cup corn sirup
¼ teaspoon salt
1¼ cups water
½ teaspoon vanilla

Cook—all but vanilla—over low heat, stirring until smooth. Add vanilla, cool and store, covered, in the refrigerator.

Mint Sirup

1 bunch fresh mint
1 cup sugar
1½ cups water

Cook sugar and water 10 minutes and pour over bruised mint. Let cool and strain out mint. Or use ½ a bunch of mint: cool the sirup first and put it into the blender with the mint for a 30-second whirl. Keep this in the refrigerator. Good with all tea-base drinks.

FRUIT AND VEGETABLE JUICE DRINKS

Fresh Apple Cocktail
(For 2)

One of the best of all; the fresh apple flavor is wonderful!

¼ cup water
1 tablespoon lemon juice
1 teaspoon sugar
1 sizable eating apple, cored and cut up (don't pare it)
½ cup cracked ice

Blend until the apple is liquefied. You may need to vary the lemon juice and sugar, depending on the kind of apples you use. Crisp fall apples like Jonathans, McIntoshes, Baldwins are good. Early apples may take more sugar, late apples more lemon juice.

Apricot Coconut Flip

(3 to 4 servings)

Exotic!

Blend 1 minute and strain through fine sieve or cheesecloth
    1½ cups shredded coconut
    1½ cups water
Return to blender and add
    ¾ cup apricot nectar
    2 teaspoons lemon juice
    1 egg white
    ½ cup cracked ice
Blend 30 seconds.

Carrot and Pineapple Cocktail

(4 servings)

A good appetizer.

    1½ cups pineapple juice
    2 medium-sized carrots, cut in pieces
    1 tablespoon lemon juice or 1 thick slice pared lemon
Have ingredients cold so that you needn't add ice. Blend until carrot is thoroughly liquefied. This looks good and tastes good. You can add ½ banana, a small cored and cut-up apple, or about ¼ bunch of water cress to make cocktails of varying flavors.

Carrot Milk

(2 or more drinks)

Good for the small fry!

    1 cup milk
    2 medium-sized carrots, cut in pieces
Blend until liquefied. This drink has an attractive pale-carrot tint and a coconut flavor, which is rather surprising.

Cherry Freeze

(For 3)

Warm-afternoon refresher.

2 cups canned cherry juice
1 tablespoon lemon juice
2 scoops vanilla ice cream

Blend until smooth. Fill the tall glasses with sparkling water.

Cranberry Cocktail

(4 servings)

One of the best of appeteasers.

2 cups raw cranberries
1 cup water
1 cup orange juice
½ cup sugar
Dash of salt

Blend until liquefied, strain and chill before serving.

Cranberry Punch Number One

(For 6)

An appetizer.

1 cup jellied cranberry sauce (whole berries or
   strained)
1 strip outer rind of orange, about 2 inches long
1 cup grape juice
1 cup orange juice
1 cup cracked ice

Blend about 20 seconds. To make a tall drink of this, fill tall glasses about two-thirds full and add ginger ale plus ice cubes.

Cranberry Punch Number Two

(8 servings, tall glasses; more in punch cups)

An attractive holiday drink.

1-pound can jellied cranberry sauce

½ cup lemon juice
1 cup orange juice
1½ teaspoons almond extract

Blend thoroughly and pour over cracked ice in punch bowl. Add a pint or more of ginger ale, or a quart of Rhine wine. Or put the cranberry mixture into tall glasses with ice cubes and fill with ginger ale or sparkling water. No, that isn't too much almond extract!

Garnish either of the cranberry punches with mint if you have it.

Grapefruit Flip

(2 drinks in champagne or sherbet glasses)

Nice for the teetotalers at a cocktail party.

¾ cup grapefruit juice
2 tablespoons lemon juice
1 tablespoon grenadine sirup
1 egg white
½ cup cracked ice

Blend until frothy; don't overdo it.

Lemonade

(1 tall glass)

The people's choice.

1 jigger (1½ ounces) lemon juice (this usually is one lemon)
1 jigger Simple Sirup (page 138)
½ cup cracked ice

Blend a few seconds; leave ice in. Pour into tall glass and fill with plain water or sparkling water. Garnish with mint sprig and cherry.

Pink Lemonade

Use the preceding recipe, but add ¼ cup red fruit juice, such as cherry or loganberry, or whirl ½ cup slightly sweetened strawberries with the drink.

Lemonade Freeze

Blend a scoop of lemon sherbet or vanilla ice cream with plain lemonade before adding the water.

Limeade

(1 tall glass)

July's best drink.

　　Juice of 3 limes
　　2 tablespoons sugar
　　½ cup cracked ice
Blend a few seconds, pour into tall glass with more cracked ice and fill with water. Garnish with cherry and mint.

Love Apple Cocktail

(4 servings)

First course at dinner.

　　1½ cups tomato juice
　　½ cup evaporated milk
　　¼ teaspoon celery salt
　　¼ teaspoon salt
　　　Dash black pepper
　　½ cup cracked ice
Blend until smooth and frothy.

Melon Cocktail

(For 2)

So delicious!

　　1 cup pineapple juice
　　1 cup diced cantaloupe, honeydew or other melon
　　1 tablespoon lemon juice
Have ingredients very cold and blend until melon is liquefied. Garnish with mint.

Watermelon Juice

You can drink your watermelon if you remove the seeds and let the blender convert the melon to liquid. No juice or water needed. This is a delicious pink drink—pure watermelon.

Orange Flip

(4 servings)

Drink your breakfast!

> 1 can frozen orange juice
> 2¼ cups water
> 2 or 3 eggs
> 2 tablespons sugar
> Dash salt

Blend 20 seconds or so. These are tall glasses.

Orange Coconut Flip

(4 to 6 servings)

There's something about that coconut flavor!

Simmer for 10 minutes, covered
> 1½ cups shredded coconut
> 3 cups water

Cool, strain and add
> 1 can frozen orange juice
> 1 cup cracked ice

Blend about 15 seconds. Pour over more cracked ice in tall glasses.

Orange Frosted

(4 to 6 servings)

Another wonderful trick with frozen juice.

> 1 can frozen orange juice
> 2¼ cups water
> 1 pint vanilla ice cream or pineapple sherbet

Blend 30 seconds to a minute. Serve in tall glasses.

Pineapple Juice Drink

(For 2)

Oh, so good and refreshing!

        ¼ cup water or orange juice
        2 cups diced fresh pineapple
        2 tablespoons sugar or ¼ cup Simple Sirup
            (page 138) or Mint Sirup (page 139)
        1 cup cracked ice
Blend to a smooth liquid. Then there's a fresh pineapple **freeze**
made by adding a couple of scoops of ice cream to this.

Pineapple Fizz

(4 servings)

Frothy, white and pleasant.

        1 cup pineapple juice
        1 tablespoon lemon juice
        1 egg white
            Dash Worcestershire sauce or bitters
        1 cup cracked ice
Blend and pour into tall glases. Fill with sparkling **water or**
ginger ale.

Pineapple Mint Freeze

(1 drink)

Smooth perfection!

        2 to 4 sprigs fresh mint
        1 cup pineapple juice
        1 scoop lemon sherbet
Blend until thick and smooth.

Pineapple Smash

(1 glass)

You can do this with any fruit juice.

        1 cup pineapple juice

1 banana, in pieces
½ cup cracked ice
Blend until banana is liquefied.

Pineapple Water Cress Cocktail

(4 or more appetizer drinks)

Lovely green, and DEE-licious!

2 cups pineapple juice
1 bunch water cress, washed, of course
3 tablespoons sugar
1 thick slice peeled lemon or
  2 tablespoons lemon juice
1 cup cracked ice
Blend until cress is reduced to drinkability.

Prune and Apple Juice

(4 or more small glasses)

This will be a favorite breakfast drink at your house, I think.

1 cup pitted prunes, with juice
1 cup apple juice
1 tablespoon lemon juice
Have ingredients chilled and blend until smooth. If this is too thick for you, add more apple juice or some orange juice.

Raspberry Punch

(12 or more servings)

Or use loganberry or cherry juice.

1½ cups raspberry juice
½ cup lemon juice
1 cup orange juice
½ cup sugar
½ small cucumber, diced
1 quart sparkling water

Blend all but sparkling water until cucumber is liquefied. Let stand in refrigerator several hours. Strain over block of ice and add charged water.

Rhubarb Punch

(8 to 10 servings)

Unusual, and very good.

Cook until tender, then chill
> 3 cups diced pink rhubarb
> 1 cup sugar
> 3 cups water

Blend ½ at a time until rhubarb is liquefied. Pour over ice in punch bowl and add
> 1 cup pineapple juice
> 1 pint ginger ale
> 3 tablespoons lemon juice

Tomato Sauerkraut Cocktail

(For 3)

Zesty and robust; a good appetizer.

> 1 cup tomato juice
> ½ cup packed sauerkraut, with juice
> 1 thin slice onion
> 3 or 4 sprigs parsley
> 1 cup cracked ice

Blend until vegetables are liquefied.

Tomato and Orange Cocktail

(5 servings)

Quite different!

> 2 cups tomato juice
> ½ cup orange juice
> 2 tablespoons lemon juice
> 2 or 3 sprigs parsley

1 teaspoon sugar
1 slice onion
¼ teaspoon salt
    Dash celery salt
1 cup cracked ice
Blend until vegetables are liquefied.

Vegetable Cocktail

(4 or 5 appetizer drinks)

A real tantalizer!

2 cups tomato juice
1 small stalk celery, with leaves, cut up
2 or 3 sprigs parsley
2 slices lemon, with peel
1 slice green pepper
1 slice onion
¼ teaspoon salt
½ teaspoon sugar
1 cup cracked ice
Blend until vegetables are completely liquefied.

COFFEE, CHOCOLATE AND TEA DRINKS

I am not going to tell you how to make coffee, chocolate and tea. You already know how. But maybe you don't know how many delicious beverages the blender will perfect, beginning with these staples. Some of them would be impossible to make without a blender.

Coffee and Chocolate

Cinnamon Coffolate

(2 tall ones)

Coffee, chocolate and cinnamon are a harmonious threesome.

1 ounce unsweetened chocolate, melted

1 cup cold strong coffee
1 cup cold milk
1½ tablespoons sugar (more if you like sweet drinks)
    Few grains salt
¼ teaspoon cinnamon
1 cup cracked ice

Blend about 30 seconds. Serve topped with whipped cream and a sprinkle of cinnamon.

Coffee Carrousel

(One 12-ouncer)

You could flavor this with real rum.

½ cup cold strong coffee
½ cup milk
1 tablespoon sugar
⅛ teaspoon rum extract
2 tablespoons (big ones) chocolate ice cream

Blend 30 seconds. If this is for a party, float more ice cream on top and stick a tiny opened paper parasol into the ice cream.

Coffee Flip

(2 tall drinks or 4 short ones)

With cream and ginger.

2 cups strong fresh coffee, chilled
¼ cup cream
¼ cup confectioners' sugar
¼ teaspoon ginger
1 egg white

Blend about 15 seconds and pour over cracked ice in glasses. Or you can whirl a cup of cracked ice with the drink.

Coffee Peach Fluff

(1 tall drink)

Delectable!

½ cup cold strong coffee

¼ cup lightly thawed quick-frozen peaches
1 tablespoon sugar
1 egg white
Few drops vanilla or almond extract

Blend 30 seconds. Put an ice cube into the glass. Best when *very* cold.

Frosted Coffee

(For 2)

Thick and creamy.

2 cups freshly made chilled coffee
1 pint vanilla ice cream

Blend until thick and fluffy.

Frosted Coffee

(For 2)

Different version.

1 tablespoon soluble coffee
¼ cup sugar
½ cup water
Few grains salt
½ cup top milk or light cream
½ pint vanilla ice cream

Blend, pour and fill glasses with carbonated water.

Iced Caramel Cream Coffee

(For 2)

There's something about that burnt sugar flavor!

¼ cup Caramel Sirup (page 138)
2 cups strong, fresh coffee, chilled
½ cup cream
1 cup cracked ice

Blend just a few seconds. This lily could be gilded with whipped cream.

Iced Mocha

(4 servings)

You won't get thin on this!

½ cup Chocolate or Cocoa Sirup (pages 138, 139)
    or canned chocolate sirup
2 cups chilled milk
½ cup cream
½ cup strong coffee, chilled
    Whipped cream (for garnish)

Blend all but whipped cream until foamy, pour over cracked ice in tall glasses and garnish with whipped cream.

Malted Coffee

(2 tall ones)

Simple and simply delicious!

3 tablespoons malted-milk powder, plain or chocolate
1 cup strong coffee
⅓ cup sugar
¾ cup milk
¼ cup cream
1 cup cracked ice

Blend until frothy—just a few seconds.

Mocha Mint Cooler

(1 drink)

Not too many calories!

½ cup cold strong coffee
¼ cup cold water
3 tablespoons Chocolate Sirup (page 138)
3 tablespoons nonfat dry milk
8 fresh mint leaves
    Mint sprig for garnish

Blend all but garnish 30 seconds, pour into glass (8 ounce) and garnish with mint. This one isn't bad even with dried mint—if you haven't any fresh.

Saigon Sip

(For 2)

Unusual and pleasing.

1 cup cold strong coffee
½ pint vanilla ice cream
2 tablespoons heavy cream
¼ teaspoon cinnamon
½ teaspoon or more sirup from preserved ginger
Whipped cream for garnish
Chopped ginger for garnish

Blend everything but the garnish for 30 seconds. You can skip the ginger in the drink and use candied ginger to decorate your whipped-cream topping if you'd rather. Chop the ginger fine.

Chocolate and Cocoa

The blender is perfect for thoroughly mixing and giving a froth to these drinks.

To make hot chocolate or cocoa, rinse the blender container with hot water. Pour your heated chocolate or cocoa into it, give it a whirl and turn into cups. Or, if necessary, turn back into the saucepan to reheat slightly. The drink will keep its froth.

Marshmallows are a good sweetener for chocolate and cocoa, and may be blended in a hot or cold drink.

It isn't necessary to melt chocolate for an iced drink. Right there you can save a step and a pan to wash.

Hot Marshmallow Cocoa

(2 servings)

An old treat in a new form.

Cook 2 or 3 minutes, stirring
2 tablespoons sugar
2 tablespoons cocoa
½ cup water
Add and heat thoroughly
1½ cups milk
Dash salt

Pour into warm blender container and blend a minute with
>   4 marshmallows

Iced Mint Chocolate

(3 tall ones)

*Very chocolatey, and absolutely no "canned"
milk taste; rich and delicious!*

Cut into small pieces, into the blender
>   2 1-ounce squares chocolate

Add
>   ½ cup sugar
>   ½ cup hot water

Blend a minute, then add
>   ¼ teaspoon salt
>   1 can (13 ounces) evaporated milk
>   ¼ teaspoon vanilla
>   ¼ teaspoon peppermint flavoring, or 4 or 5 sprigs
>   fresh mint
>   1 cup cracked ice

Keep hand on blender cover when you start the motor as this is
a full load. Blend about a minute. Serve in tall glasses. Whipped
cream or a small spoonful of ice cream may be used for garnish
if you wish.

Mexican Chocolate

(For 3)

Nice with spice.

Blend just a few seconds
>   4 tablespoons cocoa mix
>   ¼ teaspoon cinnamon
>   1 egg white

Scald and add gradually to blender contents
>   3 cups milk

Keep hand on cover to avoid a splashover. Blend until frothy
and pour back into pan in which you scalded the milk; then
heat. For chocolate milk shakes and malted milks see pages
157, 158.

Tea Drinks

Currant Tea Punch

(4 tall glasses)

Like pink tea?

1 cup currant jelly
1 cup strong cold tea
¼ cup lemon juice
½ cup orange or pineapple juice
1 cup cracked ice

Blend 15 seconds, pour into glasses, fill with sparkling water and garnish with mint sprigs if you have them.

Frosted Tea

(For 2)

Better than it sounds.

1 cup strong cold tea
½ pint lemon, lime, orange or pineapple sherbet

Blend just a few seconds, until thick and foamy, pour into glasses and fill with ginger ale. Garnish with mint or a cherry.

Iced Tea Hollywood

(For 2)

Drink your cherries.

2 cups strong cold tea
2 tablespoons lime or lemon juice
4 maraschino cherries
2 teaspoons sugar
1 cup cracked ice

Blend and pour into glasses with more ice. Put a couple of mint sprigs into the blender with this drink if you wish.

Tea Shake

(For 2)

Tea with lemon—and an egg.

1 cup strong black tea
2 tablespoons lemon or lime juice
2 teaspoons sugar
1 egg
1 cup cracked ice

Blend just a few seconds, strain or not. Good addition: a teaspoon of ginger sirup. Or replace the sugar with 2 tablespoons Mint Sirup, page 139.

THE MILK BAR

Apricot Shake

(For 2)

Equally good with fresh or dried fruit.

1 cup canned apricots or ½ cup cooked dried apricots
1 cup milk
    Few drops almond extract
½ pint vanilla ice cream

Blend until thick and fluffy.

Orange Buttermilk

(For 2)

Even if you don't care much for buttermilk, you should like this refresher.

½ cup orange juice
2 tablespoons sugar
    Inch-square piece of outer rind of orange
1½ cups buttermilk

Blend about 20 seconds. Try this with yogurt too—delicious!

Grape Buttermilk Punch
(2 drinks)

A little sweet, a little sharp.

¼ cup grape juice
2 tablespoons lemon juice
1 pint buttermilk
2 tablespoons sugar
Blend about 15 seconds.

Danish Buttermilk Drink
(For 2)

Just tart enough.

2 tablespoons sugar
1 egg
1 pint buttermilk
1 tablespoon lemon juice
Square inch of pared outer rind of lemon
Run the blender for about 20 seconds.

Caramel or Maple Egg Shake
(2 servings)

Sweet and lovely!

3 tablespoons Caramel Sirup (page 138) or
maple sirup, or brown sugar
Few grains salt
1 egg
2 cups milk
¼ teaspoon vanilla
Blend 15 to 20 seconds.

Coffee Milk Shake
(2 servings)

More nutritious than iced coffee.

2½ teaspoons instant coffee

4 teaspoons sugar
2 cups chilled milk

Blend about 10 seconds.

Coffee Rum Float

Use the preceding recipe, adding 1 tablespoon rum or ¾ teaspoon rum extract and top each glassful with a spoonful of whipped cream or ice cream.

Mocha Frosted

Use the same recipe—Coffee Milk Shake—but cut the sugar to 2 teaspoons and add ½ pint chocolate ice cream. This serves three instead of two.

Chocolate Malted Milk

(1 glass)

A teenagers' joy.

1 cup cold milk
2 tablespoons malted milk
2 tablespoons Chocolate Sirup (page 138) **or**
   1½ tablespoons sweet cocoa mix
1 scoop ice cream

Blend until thick and fluffy. Add an egg for an egg malt and, perhaps, a few drops of vanilla.

Chocolate Shake with Banana

(For 2)

Let the young ones make it themselves.

2 cups milk
1 egg
1 banana, cut in pieces
¼ cup Chocolate Sirup (page 138)
   Few grains salt

Blend about a minute. This is good with ½ Chocolate Sirup, ½ Caramel Sirup, too. And with ½ coffee and ½ milk.

Chocolate Sherry Shake

(For 2)

Enough wine to flavor—not enough to put you in a tizzy!

2 teaspoons sugar
2 cups milk
6 tablespoons chocolate malted milk
¼ cup sherry wine

Blend until frothy and serve in tall glasses with a whipped-cream garnish. You could use 3 tablespoons plain malted milk and 3 tablespoons Chocolate Sirup (page 138), no sugar. Very malty, very chocolatey.

Mint Chocolate Shake

(1 glass)

It's made before you can say shake.

1 cup milk
2 tablespoons Chocolate Sirup (page 138)
2 or 3 drops peppermint extract

Blend about 10 seconds.

Mocha Malted

(1 serving)

That delightful twosome, coffee and chocolate, again.

2 tablespoons chocolate malted milk
1 teaspoon soluble coffee
1 cup milk
1 scoop vanilla, chocolate or coffee ice cream

Blend until fluffy. A pinch of cinnamon wouldn't hurt.

Cranberry Nog

(For 2)

Colorful, and good for you.

1 cup whole or strained cranberry sauce
1 tablespoon lemon juice
1 egg
1 cup milk

Blend until smooth and top with whipped cream and nutmeg.
Everything in this drink should be cold to start with, of course.

Jam Shake

(For 1)

Youngsters love this for after school.

2 tablespoons strawberry jam or
  apricot or cherry preserves
1 cup cold milk
  Dash nutmeg

Blend about 10 seconds.

Milk Fruit Shrub

(1 tall one)

An old-timer, modernized.

½ cup any fresh berries
1 to 3 tablespoons sugar
1 tablespoon lemon juice
3 tablespoons orange juice
  Few grains salt
1 cup cold milk

Blend 30 seconds to 1 minute.

Orange Milk

(2 glasses)

Good for the youngsters.

    1 cup orange juice
    1 cup milk
    2 teaspoons sugar

Blend just a few seconds. An egg will turn this into orange egg
nog, and then a sprinkle of nutmeg is appropriate. Or fancy it
up by adding a scoop or two of orange sherbet.

Peach or Pear Shake

(For 1)

There's no season for canned fruit.

    2 halves of canned pears or peaches
    5 ounces milk
    2 tablespoons sirup from canned fruit
    2 small scoops vanilla ice cream

Blend about 15 seconds.

Fresh Peach Shake

(For 2)

This one's double peachy!

    1 cup diced fresh peaches
    ¼ cup Simple Sirup (page 138)
    2 tablespoons lemon juice
    1 cup milk
    1 cup vanilla ice cream

Blend until thick and fluffy.

Peppermint Milk

(1 glass)

Pretty pink and minty; should be very cold.

    1 cup cold milk

2 sticks peppermint candy, broken in pieces

Blend about 15 seconds. I made this with buttermilk by mistake once and have frequently made it that way on purpose, since. We use the Christmas tree's candy canes this way.

Pineapple Smoothie

(For 2)

The flavor is tropical.

1 cup fresh diced pineapple
2 tablespoons sugar
1 cup milk
½ cup cracked ice

Blend about 30 seconds to a minute.

Prune Milk

(1 tall drink)

Try this for breakfast.

¼ cup cooked pitted prunes, packed in cup
1 cup milk
Few drops vanilla or sprinkle of cinnamon
½ cup cracked ice

Blend until prunes are liquefied. This is good with an egg, too, or a scoop of ice cream.

Rennet Milk Shake

(For 1)

Silken textured.

2 tablespoons rennet powder
1 cup cold milk

Blend 15 seconds. Add a scoop of ice cream, if you like, or ½ banana. If you make the drink with chocolate rennet powder, add a few drops peppermint extract. To make more readily digestible, let stand 15 minutes before serving.

SODAS MADE IN THE BLENDER

These are even better than orthodox sodas. You simply put the ice cream, flavoring and a little milk or fruit juice in the blender, blend just a few seconds, until thick, pour it into a soda glass and fill with sparkling water. The following recipe will serve as a pattern for any fruit soda.

Strawberry Soda

(For 1)

A pink delight!

⅓ cup frozen or crushed sweetened strawberries
1 large scoop vanilla or strawberry ice cream
3 tablespoons milk or sparkling water
Blend 20 seconds or until smooth and thick, pour into glass and fill with sparkling water.

Strawberry Milk

(For 2)

So pretty and so good!

½ package frozen strawberries or 1 pint fresh
strawberries plus ¼ cup sugar
1½ cups milk
Blend about 30 seconds.

Strawberry Shake

Add 2 big scoops of vanilla ice cream to the preceding recipe.

Strawberry Malted

Add the ice cream plus ¼ cup plain malted milk.

Entrees

The blender's ability to combine ingredients and reduce them to fine particles for a sauce carries over to the preparation of many entrees. In a few cases, the blender is useful in actually mincing food to a paste, as demonstrated by the recipe for Halibut Mousse. Curries and spaghetti sauces are so much quicker and easier if you let the blender help.

This collection of recipes will show you the way to easier preparation of many main dishes and perhaps will encourage you to undertake a few recipes that otherwise might seem like too much work.

Beef and Noodle Mélange

(8 servings)

Your dinner, all in one pot.

Place in blender
  ¼ cup liquid from stuffed olives
  ½ cup stuffed olives
  1 clove garlic
  1 green pepper, diced
  1 onion, quartered
Blend until finely chopped. In a skillet brown
  1 pound ground beef in 2 tablespoons oil
Add blended sauce and
  ½ pound cheese, diced
  ¼ pound noodles, cooked
  1 No. 2 can whole-kernel corn
  1 No. 2 can tomatoes
  Salt, pepper as needed
Turn into greased casserole. Cover and bake 45 minutes at 350°.

Brazil Nut Stuffing

(For a 10-pound turkey)

A different kind of dressing.

Crumb, a broken slice at a time, and empty blender container into bowl
>15 slices white bread

Chop in ¼-cup lots and turn into bowl
>2 cups whole Brazil nuts

Place in blender container
>¼ cup water or stock
>2 stalks celery with tops, sliced
>2 small onions, quartered
>1 tablespoon salt
>1 teaspoon poultry seasoning
>½ cup melted butter

Blend until vegetables are coarsely chopped. Mix with crumbs and nuts, and stuff bird. This is a light fluffy dressing with lots of flavor.

Broiled Chicken with Mushroom Sauce

(4 or 8 servings)

The sauce makes the dish.

Brush well with butter and broil about 20 minutes on each side
>2 young broiler chickens, split or quartered

Season with salt and pepper. Place in blender
>2 cups chicken stock or bouillon
>½ medium-sized onion, cut in pieces
>¼ cup flour
>1 teaspoon salt (less if stock is salty)
>⅛ teaspoon pepper
>1 teaspoon lemon juice
>1 slice outer rind of lemon

Blend until onion is chopped fine. Sauté 5 minutes
>½ pound fresh mushrooms, washed and dried, in
>¼ cup butter or margarine

Add to blender and switch on motor for just a few seconds to chop mushrooms rather coarsely. Turn mixture into top of double boiler and cook over direct heat until thickened, stirring constantly. Add

2 tablespoons sherry

Keep hot over hot water. Serve with chicken.

Southern Chicken Loaf

(12 servings)

Best hot, but good cold, too.

Break crackers into blender a few at a time, emptying container frequently, until you have

2 cups cracker crumbs

Turn into a bowl. In the blender container place

½ onion, cut in two
1 pimiento
1⅓ teaspoons salt
1⅓ teaspoons chili powder
1⅓ cups chicken stock
1⅓ cups milk
3 eggs

Blend until vegetables are chopped. Pour over

4 cups diced cooked chicken

Add crumbs and pack into well-greased loaf pan. Set pan in another pan of hot water and bake at 350° about an hour. Serve with cream sauce to which you've added ¼ cup sliced pimiento olives.

Chili Pot Roast

(4 or more servings)

A flavorful way of fixing a less expensive cut of beef.

Place in blender

1 cup water
1 clove garlic
¼ cup packed parsley

¼ cup chili sauce
½ teaspoon Worcestershire sauce

Blend 30 seconds. Brown on all sides

3 pounds beef chuck in
3 tablespoons drippings

Season with

2½ teaspoons salt
¼ teaspoon pepper

Add ¼ cup of the blended sauce, cover and cook over low heat
or in 325° oven about 3 hours, adding remaining sauce from time
to time. Remove meat to hot platter and thicken sauce for gravy.
This can be done by blender-mixing flour and water as thickening (2 tablespoons flour per cup of total liquid).

Codfish Delight

(6 servings)

Cod in a cheese custard.

Run cold water for 15 minutes over

2 cups salt codfish

Cover with cold water and heat slowly to the boiling point, drain
and repeat 2 or 3 times to soften fish and remove excess salt.
Shred. Meanwhile, in blender container place

2⅔ cups milk
2 tablespoons butter
1 slice onion
2 eggs
1 slice green pepper
½ cup diced cheese

Blend about 20 seconds and combine with fish in buttered casserole. Mix in

1 cup blender-made crumbs (2 slices bread)

Top with

½ cup blender-made crumbs (1 slice bread)
2 tablespoons melted butter

Bake in pan of hot water at 350° for 40 minutes.

Croquettes

(4 servings)

Leftovers with a fresh-cooked taste.

Chop fine in blender, adding a few pieces at a time
>1 cup diced cooked meat, chicken or fish

Turn into bowl with
>½ cup blender-chopped cooked vegetables:
>green beans, carrots—anything you may have in the
>way of leftovers

Crumb fine in blender and add to meat and vegetables
>1 slice bread, torn apart

Place in blender container
>1 cup milk
>½ teaspoon salt
>¼ teaspoon pepper
>¼ cup flour
>1 slice onion
>4 sprigs parsley

Blend a few seconds, turn into a saucepan and cook and stir to a very thick sauce. Add to meat mixture, spread on a plate and chill. Shape into 8 croquettes. Roll in
>Fine dry crumbs (can be made in blender)

Dip in
>1 egg, slightly beaten

Dip again into crumbs and fry in deep hot fat at 375° until brown. Serve plain or with White Sauce (page 212), Jiffy Cheese Sauce (page 214) mushroom or tomato sauce. Croquettes can be fried in shallow fat but aren't so evenly crisp-coated and tempting.

Halibut Mousse

(8 servings)

This is an elegant entree for a very special luncheon.

Remove skin and bones from
>3-pound halibut steak

Simmer skin and bones for ½ hour with

> 1 teaspoon salt
> 4 peppercorns
> 1 bay leaf
> 2 cups water

Meanwhile, take a sharp knife to the raw fish and cut it into large dice. Measure

> 1 cup cream

Place ⅓ of the cream and ⅓ of the fish in the blender container at a time, and mix to a thick paste. This will require stopping the motor frequently to work the mixture down with your rubber spatula. It is best to start with just 2 or 3 cubes of fish, adding the others gradually. To the last batch of cream and fish add

> 1½ teaspoons salt
> ¼ teaspoon white pepper

Turn minced fish into bowl and add

> 4 slices bread, crumbed in blender
> ¼ cup sauterne or other white wine

Mix well and fold in

> 6 egg whites, beaten stiff

Turn into a well-buttered fish mold or loaf pan, cover with aluminum foil and place mold or pan in a pan of hot water. Bake at 325° for 1½ hours. Let mousse stand 10 minutes, then unmold on a deep platter and pour the following sauce over it.

Sauce for Halibut Mousse

Place in blender container

> 1 cup fish stock (from cooking bones and skin)
> ¼ cup soft butter
> ¼ cup flour
> ¼ cup packed parsley
> ½ teaspoon salt
> ¼ teaspoon pepper
> 1 egg

Blend smooth and turn into saucepan with

> 1 cup cream

Cook and stir over low heat until smooth and thick, then add

> ¼ cup white wine

Stir and cook a minute or so longer, but do not allow sauce to boil. Taste for seasoning and add more salt if you need it.

Lamb or Chicken Curry

(6 servings)

This is real curry, but not too hot.

Place in blender container
>1 cup meat stock or bouillon
>1 onion, quartered and sautéed in
>>2 tablespoons butter
>
>2 apples, sliced
>3 tablespoons flour
>2 tablespoons curry powder
>½ cup sugar
>¼ cup plum jam (or another kind)
>¼ cup chutney
>1 clove garlic

Blend until ingredients are chopped and add
>½ cup raisins

Simmer for half an hour with
>1 cup more stock

Serve over
>3 cups diced cooked lamb or chicken

Accompany with fresh grated coconut (see page 244), more chutney, chopped cashews or peanuts.

Macaroni and Cheese Mousse

(6 servings)

A variation of a standard American dish.

Cook about 12 minutes in boiling salted water and drain
>8 ounces macaroni (elbow or broken lengths)

Crumb in blender and set aside
>2 slices white bread, torn apart

Place in blender container
>3 eggs
>1½ cups milk
>1 teaspoon salt
>⅓ cup butter
>¼ cup packed parsley

> 1 small onion, in quarters
> 2 pimientos
> ½ pound American cheese, diced

Blend about 30 seconds and mix with macaroni. Add crumbs. Place in greased shallow baking dish, 9 by 12 inches, and set in a pan of hot water. Bake in moderate oven at 350° for an hour or until the custard sets. Serve plain or with a tomato sauce.

Meat Loaf Delicious

(8 or more servings)

Perfectly seasoned.

Place in blender container

> 1 egg
> ½ cup water
> 1 small onion, quartered
>   Tops from 4 or 5 stalks celery, in pieces
> 4 or 5 sprigs parsley
> 2 teaspoons salt
> ½ teaspoon sage
> ¼ teaspoon pepper

Blend until vegetables are chopped. Mix with

> 2 pounds ground beef
> ½ pound bulk pork sausage

Pack into loaf pan and bake at 350° for 1 hour and 15 minutes. This loaf is good hot or cold, and it can be sliced into neat, thin slices when cold, so the leftovers are fine for Sunday night.

Nutburgers

(4 to 6 servings)

A vegetarian treat!

Crumb in blender and turn into bowl

> 3 slices bread, torn apart

Place in blender container

> 1 cup milk
> 1 egg
> 1 slice onion

¼ cup packed parsley
1½ teaspoons salt
2 cups pecans or walnuts

Blend until nuts are chopped fairly fine. Add to crumbs and shape into 8 or 12 patties. Brown in butter in a heavy skillet for about 5 minutes on each side. Serve with mushroom sauce. A can of condensed mushroom soup with a tablespoon or so of cream or sherry makes a good sauce.

Puffy Omelet with Cheese

(6 servings)

Perfect for brunch.

Place in blender container
⅓ cup milk or water
1 cup diced Cheddar or Swiss cheese
1 teaspoon salt
¼ teaspoon pepper
6 egg yolks
Sprig or two of parsley

Blend just a few seconds to combine ingredients well. Fold into
6 egg whites, beaten stiff

Turn into well-greased skillet or omelet pan, spread evenly and cook slowly over low heat until puffed and delicately brown underneath. Then place in moderately hot oven, 375°, to brown top. Turn out onto heated serving plate and serve with White Sauce (page 212), a creamed vegetable or creamed fish. You needn't separate white and yolks of eggs for an omelet, but you get a puffier one if you do. Of course you can crease it down the center and serve it with the filling in the middle, a standard practice in serving omelets.

Pork Chops with Cranberries

(6 servings)

A holiday season brightener.

Dredge with flour
6 inch-thick pork chops

Season with

>1½ teaspoons salt
>¼ teaspoon pepper

Brown in

>3 tablespoons drippings

Place browned chops in casserole. Place in blender

>¼ cup water
>2 cups fresh cranberries
>1 small orange, cut in pieces, peel included
>½ cup sugar

Blend until fruit is fine. Pour over chops, cover casserole and bake in moderate oven at 350° for an hour or longer, until chops are very tender.

Curried Rice Ring

(12 servings)

To hold creamed chicken, turkey or shrimps.

Place in blender container

>4 eggs
>2 cups milk
>6 tablespoons soft butter
>½ cup packed parsley
>1 teaspoon curry powder
>¼ teaspoon celery seed
>1 teaspoon salt
>⅛ teaspoon pepper

Blend until parsley is finely cut and pour over

>6 cups cooked rice seasoned with salt (1½ cups before cooking)

Stir until well mixed. Fill large greased ring mold. Set mold in a pan of hot water and bake in a moderate oven at 350° for about an hour. Cool for 5 minutes, then turn out on a hot serving platter and fill center of ring with creamed chicken, turkey or fish. This is a good buffet-supper combination. Season the chicken (or turkey) or fish sauce with a little sherry.

Rice and Nut Loaf

(6 to 8 servings)

No meat, but it tastes like meat!

Place in blender container

      1 8-ounce can tomato sauce

      1 egg

      1 stalk celery with tops, cut in pieces

      2 medium-sized onions, quartered

      4 or 5 sprigs parsley

      1 teaspoon salt

      ½ teaspoon sage

      2 tablespoons butter or oil

Blend until vegetables are cut fine. Add and blend just a second or two

      1 cup walnuts

Fold in

      1½ cups cooked rice

      1 cup cracker crumbs (can be prepared in blender)

Pour into greased loaf pan about 9½ by 5½ inches and bake at 350° for 1 hour. Serve with tomato sauce.

Deviled Salmon in Sea Shells

(6 servings)

Lemon is the secret.

Place in blender container

      1 cup canned tomato soup, **undiluted**

      ¼ onion

      ¼ green pepper, diced

      3 tablespoons butter

      ½ teaspoon salt

      1 teaspoon prepared mustard

      1 slice lemon, including peel

Blend about 15 seconds and pour over

      1 pound canned salmon, flaked

Pile in baking shells or ramekins and top with, in order,

½ cup crumbs (1 slice bread, blender-crumbed)
3 tablespoons melted butter
6 thin slices lemon (1 per serving)
Paprika

Bake at 400° about 25 minutes.

Baked Sea Food Salad

(6 servings)

Deserves its popularity.

Place in blender container
¾ cup mayonnaise
1 tablespoon Worcestershire sauce
1 tablespoon lemon juice
½ large green pepper, in pieces
2 large stalks celery, sliced
1 slice onion
½ teaspoon salt
Dash pepper

Blend until vegetables are chopped fairly fine. Add
1 cup cooked or canned shrimp
1 small can crab meat, flaked coarsely

Turn into individual greased shells. Place in blender
6 soda crackers, broken
½ cup cheese, diced

Blend until crackers and cheese form fine crumbs. Top casseroles. Bake 30 minutes in moderate oven, 350°. The mayonnaise in this combination gives it the salad name, and also makes a smooth, flavorsome binder for the fish.

Spaghetti with Burgundy Sauce

(8 servings)

This dish will make your party.

Place in blender container
3½ cups canned tomatoes (No. 2½ can)
½ teaspoon cinnamon
¼ teaspoon cloves

¼ teaspoon nutmeg

1 or 2 cloves garlic

Cover and blend 30 seconds. Turn all but a cup of the tomato sauce into a large, heavy saucepan. Add to what remains in the blender

2 large onions, cut in pieces

2 stalks celery with tops, diced

1 green pepper, cut in pieces

Blend until vegetables are chopped fairly fine and turn into saucepan with remainder of tomatoes. Sauté for about 10 minutes, until meat is brown

¼ cup oil

1 pound ground beef

½ pound sliced mushrooms

Add to sauce with

2 cans tomato paste

2½ teaspoons salt

1 tablespoon sugar

1 cup Burgundy or other red wine

Simmer gently for 30 minutes or longer until sauce is thick. Add just before serving

½ cup more wine

Serve over

1 pound hot cooked spaghetti

Accompany the spaghetti with garlic bread and a green salad. Keep tasting the sauce as you go along to check on the seasonings—that's the real secret of making a good spaghetti sauce.

Spaghetti Loaf with Shrimp Sauce

(8 servings)

Ready for the oven in no time.

Cook in boiling salted water until tender

1½ cups broken spaghetti

Place in blender container

1 cup milk

¼ cup butter

3 egg yolks

1 cup diced cheese

5 sprigs parsley
1 pimiento
½ small onion
1 teaspoon salt
½ teaspoon pepper

Blend thoroughly and add to spaghetti. Add

1 cup soft crumbs (2 slices bread)

Fold in

3 egg whites, beaten stiff

Turn into greased loaf pan and bake at 350° for 1 hour. Turn out
on hot platter and serve with Shrimp Sauce.

Shrimp Sauce

3 tablespoons butter or margarine
3 tablespoons flour
1½ cups milk
1 teaspoon Worcestershire sauce
½ teaspoon salt
¼ teaspoon pepper
1 cup cooked shrimp or 1 5-ounce can

Blend until shrimp is chopped. Heat in a saucepan until thickened.

Baked Stuffed Spareribs

(6 servings)

Caraway subtly seasons the dressing.

Fry until crisp

1 cup diced salt pork (½ pound)

Place in bowl and add

1 cup diced tart apple
1 cup sliced celery
12 slices bread, crumbed

In blender container place

¼ onion
2 tablespoons sugar
¼ cup packed parsley
1 teaspoon salt

¼ teaspoon pepper
¼ cup water
1 teaspoon caraway seeds

Blend about 20 seconds and add to other ingredients. Rub with salt and pepper

4 small or 2 large sides of spareribs

Bake in 350° oven 45 minutes, then drain off fat, place dressing in pan and top with ribs. Bake 1 hour longer or until tender.

Tuna with Brazil Nuts

(4 servings)

A quickie for lunch.

Cut fine in blender, a few at a time, emptying the container into a bowl

1 cup Brazil nuts

Place in blender container

¼ cup butter
2 cups milk
¼ cup flour
¾ teaspoon salt
⅛ teaspoon pepper
2 pimientos
½ teaspoon Worcestershire sauce

Blend until pimientos are coarsely cut—just a second or two—turn into saucepan and cook until thickened. Add, breaking apart

1 7-ounce can tuna

Add nuts previously prepared. Bake in small greased baking dish for 15 minutes at 350°.

Tuna Loaf

(6 to 8 servings)

A good choice for the Ladies' Aid luncheon.

Crumb in blender

8 slices bread, torn apart (1 slice at a time, emptying container between times)

Place in container

>1 can condensed mushroom soup
>1 cup milk
>½ teaspoon salt
>¼ teaspoon paprika
>2 eggs
>1 pimiento

Blend smooth and pour over crumbs and

>2 7-ounce cans tuna, flaked

Bake in greased 1½-quart loaf pan at 350° for 45 minutes. Serve with White Sauce (page 212) or mushroom sauce made with another can of the soup.

Turkey Cashew

(4 to 6 servings)

A post-Thanksgiving treat.

Crumb in blender

>1 slice white bread, broken

Turn into small bowl or cup. Place in blender and chop coarsely

>¾ cup cashews

Turn into a second cup or place on waxed paper. Place in blender container

>1 cup cream
>¼ teaspoon sage
>1½ teaspoons salt
> Dash of pepper
>¼ cup packed parsley
>2 tablespoons sherry

Blend until parsley is chopped. Scatter ½ the chopped nuts on the bottom of a greased casserole and cover with ½ of

>2 cups diced or sliced turkey

Add the rest of the nuts and the remainder of the turkey and cover with blended cream and seasonings. Top with the crumbs and a few broken cashews. Bake at 350°, moderate oven, about 25 minutes until browned.

Veal Birds

(6 servings)

The birds don't sing, but you will!

Crumb in blender

> 6 slices white bread, torn apart (blend 1 slice at a time and empty container)

Place in blender container

> ¼ cup water
> 1 onion, diced
> 1 teaspoon salt
> ¼ teaspoon pepper
> ¼ cup butter
> 4 or 5 sprigs parsley
> ½ teaspoon sage
> ½ cup diced celery

Blend until vegetables are chopped. Add to crumbs and mix well. Place this dressing on

> 1½ pounds veal cutlet, cut thin and into 6 servings

Roll up veal and skewer or tie with string. Dredge with flour and brown in

> ¼ cup drippings

Place browned birds in casserole with water or cream to cover bottom, cover tightly and bake in moderate oven at 325° for 1½ hours. Drippings may be thickened for gravy.

10

Salads, Blender-Made

It isn't practical to try cutting cabbage for slaw in your blender or to chop large amounts of carrots, celery and other vegetables. But for small amounts of chopped vegetables, the blender is very helpful. For example, you can blender-chop 2 carrots and sprinkle them over a bowl of mixed greens and tomatoes to give a pleasant crunchy effect.

When you want to sieve an avocado, grate a cucumber or mash a banana for a molded salad, the blender is your devoted slave. Presto! There's your mixture! The blender is also a speedy mixer of seasonings for an aspic or cream cheese as a base for a frozen fruit salad.

A temptation to resist is the one that would have us mince many vegetables very fine for salads. Salads should have texture and crispness; they shouldn't resemble baby food.

Molded Asparagus and Egg Salad

(6 servings)

Use fresh tips of asparagus if you can.

Soften
  1 tablespoon plain gelatin in
   ¼ cup cold water
Dissolve in
  1 cup boiling water from asparagus
Place in blender container with
  ½ teaspoon salt
  1 slice onion
  1 pimiento
  1 tablespoon lemon juice
  ½ cup diced celery

Blend until ingredients are chopped fine. Chill until mixture begins to thicken and add

> 3 hard-cooked eggs, diced
> 2 cups diced cooked asparagus
> 1 cup mayonnaise

Turn into large oiled mold; chill until firm and unmold on greens. Garnish with tomato quarters. Accompany with Basic French Dressing (page 192).

Party Avocado Mold

(10 to 12 servings)

Pleasingly tart; delectable!

Soften

> 2 tablespoons plain gelatin in
> ½ cup cold orange juice

Dissolve over hot water and place in blender container with

> 1½ cups more orange juice (or juice and water)
> 1 tablespoon sugar
> 1 teaspoon salt
> 2 tablespoons pickle relish
> ⅓ cup lemon juice
> Few drops tabasco sauce
> 1 thin slice onion
> 3 avocados, diced

Blend smooth and turn into large ring mold or individual molds and chill until firm. Turn out on greens and fill center of ring with orange and grapefruit sections. Accompany with mayonnaise. This is the perfect buffet-party salad.

Jellied Beet Salad

(6 servings)

Beautiful color in this salad; piquant flavor.

Place in blender container

> 1 package lemon gelatin
> 1 cup hot beet juice (from No. 2 can), and water

Blend a few seconds to dissolve gelatin. Add

¼ large lemon (no seeds)
1 teaspoon salt
½ small onion
1 tablespoon horse-radish

Blend until ingredients are liquefied. Add

No. 2 can beets, well drained

Blend until beets are chopped, not too fine. Turn into ring mold.
Place in blender container

½ cup water
2 carrots, sliced
Tops of 2 celery stalks, cut in pieces

Blend until chopped. Add to beets in ring mold. Stir to mix.
Chill until firm and serve with sour cream or mayonnaise and
sour cream combined. Curly endive, with its contrasts of light
and dark green, is a pretty garnish.

Chicken Salad in Sherry Aspic

(Serves 10 at a buffet)

The wine makes it an aristocrat.

Soften

2 tablespoons plain gelatin in
½ cup cold chicken stock or chicken bouillon

Dissolve over hot water. Turn into blender container and add

½ cup diced or sliced carrots
1 thickish slice medium-sized onion
½ cup diced celery
About 3 sprigs parsley
½ teaspoon salt
¼ teaspoon pepper
2 tablespoons lemon juice
¼ cup sherry wine

Blend until vegetables are finely minced. Turn into large ring
mold with

3 cups more chicken stock or bouillon
1½ cups diced cooked chicken
½ cup diced celery
½ cup cooked or canned peas

Chill until firm. Unmold on greens, and accompany with mayonnaise.

Rice and Chicken Salad

(4 servings)

If you've never had rice in a salad, you've missed something!

Mince in the blender on low speed or with quick on and off switches

>1 stalk celery, sliced
>5 stuffed olives
>½ green pepper, cut in pieces

Turn into a bowl with

>2 cups cold cooked rice
>1 small can boned chicken or turkey
>½ cup mayonnaise
>1 tablespoon chili sauce
>1 tablespoon vinegar
>1 tablespoon sugar
>1 tablespoon cream
>A little pineapple juice

Mix well. Chill in custard cups and turn each salad out onto a ring of pineapple placed on lettuce. Garnish with a dab of mayonnaise and a slice of stuffed olive for each. The rice stretches the good chicken flavor and gives a nice texture.

Crab Meat Salad

(8 servings)

Shrimps are good this way, too.

Soften

>2 tablespoons plain gelatin in
>½ cup cold water

Dissolve in

>1 cup hot condensed tomato soup

Cool and turn into blender with

>½ pound cream cheese
>1½ cups diced celery
>1 large green pepper, in pieces
>1 slice onion
>1 cup mayonnaise

Blend until vegetables are chopped fine. Chill until slightly thickened and fold in contents of

> 1 6½-ounce can crab meat

Turn into oiled mold and chill until firm. Unmold on greens and serve with mayonnaise.

Cranberry Jewel Salad

(6 servings)

A high-carat ruby.

Dissolve

> 1 package raspberry gelatin in
> 1¼ cups boiling water

Cool somewhat and turn into blender with

> 1 orange, cut in pieces (seeds removed, but
>   not the peel)
> 1 can whole or jellied cranberry sauce

Blend until orange is finely chopped. Add

> ¼ cup port wine

Chill mixture in individual molds or 1 large one until firm. Serve on crisp lettuce.

Cranberry Relish Salad

(6 servings)

Place in blender container

> 1 package lemon-flavored gelatin
> 1 cup hot water

Blend a few seconds to dissolve gelatin and add

> 1 orange, quartered (seeds removed but not the peel)
> 1½ cups cranberries
> 1 apple, cored and sliced
> 1 cup sugar
> ¼ teaspoon salt

Blend until fruits are finely chopped. Add and blend for just a second

> ½ cup pecans

Turn into individual molds or into 1 large mold and chill until firm. Unmold on greens. Serve with a dressing made by combining mayonnaise and whipped cream in equal parts.

Frozen Fruit Salad

(6 servings)

Can serve as a dessert, too.

Soften
      1 teaspoon plain gelatin in
        3 tablespoons pineapple juice (from 9-ounce can
          crushed fruit)
Dissolve over boiling water and place in blender container. Add
      2 tablespoons lemon juice
      1 tablespoon maraschino cherry juice
      1 banana
        Dash of salt
      ⅓ cup mayonnaise
Blend smooth and add, with motor running
      12 marshmallows
When marshmallows are blended, fold in
      1 9-ounce can crushed pineapple
      ½ cup quartered maraschino cherries
      1 cup heavy cream, whipped
Freeze until firm in refrigerator tray. Cut into squares and
serve on crisp greens.

Ham and Potato Salad Loaf

(6 servings)

Handsomest potato salad ever!

Line small loaf pan with wax paper (extend the wax paper
up over the sides). Cover bottom and sides of pan with
      ½ pound thinly sliced baked ham
Soften
      1 tablespoon gelatin in
      ¼ cup cold water
Dissolve over hot water and place in blender container with
      1 cup mayonnaise
    1½ teaspoons salt
      1 slice onion
      3 sprigs parsley

           1 pimiento
           2 stalks celery, cut
Blend until vegetables are chopped. Add mixture to
           6 cups diced cooked potatoes
           1 cup diced ham
Turn into loaf pan over ham slices and chill until firm. **Turn out** on platter and remove paper. Cut in thick slices to serve.

Jellied Pineapple and Cucumber Salad with Chablis

(6 servings)

Has an Epicurean flavor.

Soften
           2 tablespoons plain gelatin in
            ½ cup cold water
Dissolve over hot water and turn into blender container with
           1½ cups Chablis wine
           1 cucumber, in pieces
           1 green pepper, in pieces
           1 teaspoon salt
           ½ cup sugar
           2 tablespoons lemon juice
Blend until vegetables are finely cut; chill until mixture begins to thicken, then add
           1 9-ounce can crushed pineapple
Turn into large ring mold and chill until firm. Unmold on greens and serve with mayonnaise.

Roquefort Ring

(8 servings)

Definitely a party girl!

Soften for 5 minutes
           1 tablespoon plain gelatin in
           ¼ cup sauterne wine

Dissolve over hot water. Place in blender container with

> ¼ cup more wine
> 2 tablespoons lemon juice
> ½ cup mayonnaise
> 1 thin slice onion
> ½ teaspoon Worcestershire sauce
> 1 cup crumbled Roquefort or blue cheese
> 1 3-ounce package cream cheese (soft)

Blend until smooth. Fold in

> 1 cup heavy cream, whipped
> Salt and celery salt to taste

Turn into oiled 1-quart ring mold. Chill until firm. Unmold on water cress, romaine or other greens and fill the center of the ring wtih fresh fruit. Serve with Basic French Dressing (page 192).

Salad Luncheon

(8 large molds or 1 loaf)

Hot rolls are all you need with this delicious salad.

Soften

> 1 tablespoon gelatin in
> 2 tablespoons lemon juice

Dissolve over hot water and place in blender with

> 1 cup warm water
> 1 avocado, peeled, seed removed
> 1 cup diced celery
> ½ cup mayonnaise
> 1 teaspoon salt
> 1 slice onion

Blend until celery is finely chopped. Chill until slightly thickened and fold in

> 1 cup diced cooked corned beef or ham
> ¼ cup diced pimiento
> ¼ cup diced green pepper
> 2 diced hard-cooked eggs
> 2 cups cooked macaroni

Chill in individual 5-ounce molds or loaf pan until firm. Unmold on greens.

Sardine Stuffed Egg Salad

(4 servings)

Just fancy deviled eggs.

Hard cook
>   4 eggs

Cut lengthwise into halves and put yolks into blender container with
>   1 thin slice small onion
>   ⅓ teaspoon salt
>   ¼ teaspoon pepper
>   2 tablespoons chili sauce
>   2 tablespoons mayonnaise
>   2 sardines
>   2 or 3 slices cucumber
>   1 slice green pepper (optional)

Blend until ingredients are finely chopped. Pile filling into egg whites. Chill and serve on lettuce with Basic French Dressing (page 192).

Shrimp Party Salad

(6 or more servings)

A general favorite.

Soften
>   2 tablespoons plain gelatin in
>   ¾ cup cold water

Dissolve over hot water and place in blender container with
>   1½ cups water
>   ¼ cup sugar
>   6 tablespoons lemon juice
>   ¾ teaspoon salt
>   1 cup mayonnaise

Blend a few seconds and turn a little of the mixture into a ring mold to form a thin jellied layer. Chill until firm. Meanwhile, add to blender

> 1 cup cooked shrimps
> 1 cup diced celery
> 1 slice onion
> ¼ cup parsley
> 1 pimiento

Blend until ingredients are chopped fairly fine. Turn into ring mold on top of jellied layer and chill until firm. Unmold on a serving platter and garnish with greens, whole shrimps, pimiento strips. Serve with mayonnaise seasoned with a little lemon juice.

Glorified Tomato Aspic

(6 servings)

Just a little crunchiness—it's pleasant.

Place in blender container

> 1 package lemon gelatin
> 1 cup hot tomato juice

Blend a few seconds to dissolve gelatin. **Add**

> ¾ cup more tomato juice
> 2 tablespoons vinegar
> 1 thin slice onion
> 1 cup diced celery
> ¼ cup stuffed olives

Blend a few seconds to chop celery fairly fine. Add and blend until barely chopped

> 1 hard-cooked egg, quartered

Turn into individual molds (or 1 large one) and chill until firm. Unmold on greens and serve with mayonnaise.

Yogurt Garlic Salad with Cucumbers

(4 servings)

Nice for a party.

Place in container

> 2 cups yogurt

½ clove garlic, peeled

1 teaspoon salt

1 tablespoon lemon juice

Start blender and add gradually

2 cucumbers, cut in chunks

Blend until very smooth. Soften

2 tablespoons gelatin in

¼ cup of the above blender mixture

Heat to dissolve, then return to blender as it runs. Pour into 1-quart mold. Chill until firm. Add a few fresh mint leaves to this if you have them.

11

Salad Dressings

Salad dressings are so easy and so perfectly emulsified in a blender that they're fun to make, and it's nothing at all to have 6 or more different kinds on hand, neatly labeled and stored in fruit jars or bottles, to use as your fancy chooses.

Reach for the Anchovy and Roquefort, or the Celery Seed Dressing; pick a sour-cream blend for the cole slaw, a garlicky sauce for a bowl of mixed greens.

Make big batches of Basic French Dressing and Mayonnaise. With these two you can have a hundred adventures in salad-making. Add ingredients as you please—onion and garlic, chili sauce and lemon juice, capers and anchovies, cheese and parsley and water cress. You can have everything dispersed so finely in your dressing that nothing can be identified except by flavor. But if you want a salad dressing with chopped egg or onion in it, you can have that kind, too.

For most dressings, everything goes into the blender container at once. You put the cover on, rest your hand lightly on top, switch on the motor and let it run for just a few seconds. Then empty the container into the jar you wish to store the dressing in. One blender, which will operate with various sizes of Mason jars as well as with its own container, permits you to blend and store the dressing in the same jar. No extra dishwashing here!

Most of my favorite dressings are included in this collection. I hope they'll be your favorites, too.

FRENCH DRESSINGS AND VARIATIONS

This good Basic French Dressing can be varied in dozens of ways, so make a big batch while you're at it, and add other ingredients to parts of the dressing to suit your fancy.

Basic French Dressing

(1 pint)

Take off from here in any direction!

½ cup vinegar
1½ cups salad oil
1½ teaspoons salt
2 teaspoons sugar
1 slice small onion
½ teaspoon paprika
½ teaspoon mustard

Whirl in the electric blender until emulsified, ½ minute or so, and store in a covered jar in the refrigerator.

Blue Cheese Dressing

To a cup of the Basic French Dressing add ¼ pound blue cheese. Or use Roquefort (French), Gorgonzola (Italian) or the Danish blue cheese—the sharper the better. Blend until perfectly smooth, or let there be lumps, as you please.

Chutney Dressing

This is for meat salads—or for chicken or shrimp. Add as much as ¼ cup of chutney to a cup of the basic dressing. Don't blend until perfectly smooth; leave it a little bumpy.

Ginger Dressing

A cup of Basic French (*parlez-vous?*) plus 1 tablespoon preserved ginger and sirup. Good on fruits.

Lorenzo Dressing

Adds color to a salad.

1 cup Basic French Dressing
3 tablespoons chili sauce
2 or 3 green onions with tops, cut in pieces
¼ bunch water cress
½ pimiento

Blend until cress is finely chopped. Try this on French endive or chilled fresh asparagus.

Mint Dressing

Tuck about 6 sprigs of fresh mint into the blender with a cup of the Basic French Dressing (page 192) and let the motor run until the mint is in very fine particles. If for fruit salads, add a teaspoon of sugar, too.

Pecan Dressing

Subtly different, and so intriguing!

Sauté ¼ cup pecans in a little butter until browned lightly, and put into the blender for a whirl with 1 cup Basic French Dressing. Mixed greens take to this and vice versa. Perfect harmony!

Vinaigrette Dressing

(Around a cupful)

The perfect choice for asparagus.

1 cup Basic French Dressing or any good bottled one
6 stuffed olives
1 teaspoon capers
3 or 4 green onions with tops, cut in pieces
2 tablespoons pickle relish
3 or 4 sprigs parsley
1 teaspoon chervil (if you have it)

Blend until emulsified, not until perfectly smooth.

Other French-Type Dressings

Anchovy French Dressing

(A little over 1 cup)

Perfection for mixed greens.

1 small tin (2 ounces) anchovy fillets or rolled
   anchovies with capers

    ¼ teaspoon salt
    1 cup olive oil
    1 teaspoon mustard
    1 slice medium-sized onion
    ¼ cup vinegar (tarragon is good)

Use the oil in the anchovy can as well as the fish. Blend everything for a minute or so, until you get a smooth dressing which doesn't show its anchovy. (You can certainly *taste* anchovy, though!) Some people like a little more vinegar for extra sharpness—use ⅓ cup if you like. I usually make a double batch of the anchovy dressing, we like it so much. It improves on standing.

Anchovy and Beet Dressing

To the dressing above or to 1 cup Basic French Dressing add ¼ cup cooked diced beets and 2 quartered hard-cooked eggs. If you use basic dressing, you'll have to add the anchovies, naturally—6 or 8. Then blend until smooth, or just until beets, eggs, anchovies are chopped as you wish.

Anchovy and Roquefort Dressing

(Little over 1 cup)

Everybody raves over this!

    ⅔ cup olive oil or salad oil
    1 can (2 ounces) anchovies with their oil
    3 tablespoons vinegar
    3 tablespoons lemon juice
    1 sliver garlic
    ½ teaspoon each: mustard, sugar, onion salt,
        celery salt
      Dash Worcestershire
      Dash tabasco
    3-ounce wedge Roquefort-type cheese
    ¼ teaspoon paprika

Blend until perfectly smooth.

Beer Dressing

(About 1 cup)

Not bad at all on mixed greens!

½ cup olive oil
¼ teaspoon salt
1 teaspoon paprika
Thin sliver garlic
¼ teaspoon white pepper
3 tablespoons vinegar or lemon juice
2 teaspoons sugar
¼ cup beer

Put everything into the blender and blend until you can't find the garlic. You can use flat beer for this, just as you can with Welsh rabbit. The flavor's there.

Chiffonade Dressing

(1 ¼ cups)

Bright with beets.

¾ cup salad oil
¼ cup tarragon vinegar
½ teaspoon salt
1 teaspoon sugar
¼ teaspoon paprika
2 thin slices medium-sized onion
4 leafy sprigs parsley
1 hard-cooked egg, quartered
2 medium-sized beets, in pieces

Blend until the solids are in tiny pieces—chopped, rather than completely blended. This will take not much more than a switch-on, switch-off action of the motor.

Curry Dressing

(About 1 cup)

For meats, chicken, sea-food, vegetable salads.

1 teaspoon salt

1 teaspoon curry powder
1 teaspoon sugar
1 slice medium-sized onion
3 or 4 sprigs parsley
   Thin sliver garlic
2-inch strip pared outer rind of lemon
¾ cup oil
¼ cup vinegar
   Dash cayenne pepper
¼ teaspoon black pepper

Blend until smooth. You know how curry and chutney go together—well, you can add 2 tablespoons chutney to this for a wonderfully good variation.

Pimiento Salad Dressing

(Around 1 cupful)

Unusual, bright-colored—you'll like it.

Contents of a 4-ounce can pimientos (usually
   3 pimientos, plus juice)
2 tablespoons blue cheese
⅓ cup salad oil
¼ cup vinegar
1½ teaspoons sugar
½ teaspon salt
   Thin slice small onion
¼ teaspoon pepper

Blend just a few seconds until smooth. Good on vegetable salads, citrus salads.

Russian Dressing

(About 3 cups)

Pungent and flavorsome!

1 can tomato soup
1 cup tarragon vinegar
2 teaspoons salt
½ teaspoon paprika

1 tablespoon Worcestershire sauce
½ cup salad oil
¼ cup sugar
½ teaspoon pepper
½ teaspoon mustard
    Small clove garlic
    Small onion, quartered
3 tablespoons horse-radish

Blend ingredients into a smooth emulsion.

Prize Surprise Dressing

(Around 1 cupful)

This did *win a prize!*

1 hard-cooked egg yolk
1 cooked chicken liver
1 teaspoon prepared mustard
1 thin slice small onion
    Dash black pepper
3 tablespoons tarragon vinegar
¼ teaspoon salt
¾ cup olive oil

Blend until smooth.

Superb French Dressing

(3 cups)

This won a prize, too!

1 cup catsup
¼ cup sugar
½ cup vinegar (herb-flavored is nice)
1 teaspoon salt
1 small onion, quartered
½ teaspoon celery seed
¼ teaspoon paprika
¾ cup salad oil or olive oil, or ½ each

Give these ingredients a blending of about 30 seconds.

Wine Dressing

(1 ¼ cups)

For fruits or greens.

    1 teaspoon salt
    1 teaspoon sugar
    ¼ teaspoon dry mustard
       Dash pepper
    1 slice medium-sized onion
    ½ cup sauterne
    ¼ cup white vinegar
    ½ cup salad oil

Blend until emulsified.

Red Wine Dressing

(About 1 ½ cups)

For that big bowl of mixed greens and tomatoes.

    1 teaspoon sugar
    1 teaspoon salt
    ½ teaspoon mustard
    1 teaspoon Worcestershire sauce
    ¼ cup catsup
    ¼ cup Burgundy or claret
    ¼ cup red-wine vinegar
    ¾ cup olive oil
    1 clove garlic

Blend until perfectly smooth.

FRUIT SALAD DRESSINGS AND DRESSINGS MADE WITH FRUITS

Dressings for fruit salads usually are sweeter than those for vegetable salads, mixed greens and the hearty salads made with meat, fish or chicken. Most of them are attractive in appearance, too, whether color or texture is the distinguishing quality.

Avocado Dressing

(1 cup or thereabouts)

For tomato salads, citrus fruits or greens.

  1 large ripe avocado, peeled and pitted
¼ small onion
  1 medium-sized tomato, quartered
  3 tablespoons lemon juice
  1 tablespoon olive oil
  1 teaspoon salt
¼ teaspoon pepper
    Dash tabasco

Blend until smooth. Lemon protects the color of avocado. You can even use more and counteract any sourness or sharpness with a little sugar. Put in a whole pared lemon, if you like, cutting it in pieces first and removing seeds. (You can leave the seeds in if you like—I prefer to remove them.) One lemon is the equivalent, in general, of 3 to 4 tablespoons juice, depending on size.

Celery Seed Dressing

(1 pint)

Sweet and transparent-looking; the best of its kind, I think.

⅔ cup sugar
1½ teaspoons salt
  1 tablespoon paprika
½ teaspoon mustard
½ cup tarragon wine vinegar
¼ medium-sized onion
  1 cup salad oil
  1 tablespoon or more celery seed

Blend until thick and smooth.

Cherry Fruit Salad Dressing

(1 cup)

Try it on pear salad.

¼ cup lemon juice
½ cup salad oil
¼ cup maraschino or canned sweet cherry juice
6 cherries (no pits)
1 tablespoon sugar
½ teaspoon salt
½ teaspoon paprika
3 ounces cream cheese (optional; you don't need it)

Blend until smooth. If you add the cheese, you get another kind of dressing—but good! Or you could fold in whipped cream.

Cranberry Dressing

(About 1 ½ cups)

Whirr! And it's made!

1 cup cranberry jelly
¾ cup salad oil
3 tablespoons vinegar
1 teaspoon mustard
½ teaspoon salt

Blend until smooth. Pretty and good with peach and cottage-cheese salad, among others.

Cranberry Cream Dressing

(More than a cup)

A pale pink.

Blend 30 seconds
⅔ cup fresh cranberries
3 tablespoons sugar
2 tablespoons water
½ teaspoon salt

Boil for 5 minutes. Cool and blend again with

3 tablespoons salad oil

1½ tablespoons lemon juice

Fold into

⅓ cup cream, whipped until thick

Cream Cheese and Currant Dressing

(About 2 cups)

"Elegant!" you'll say.

½ cup currant jelly

3-ounce package cream cheese

3 tablespoons lemon juice

¼ teaspoon salt

Blend until smooth. Then fold in

1 cup whipped cream

3 tablespoons chopped nuts

French Fruit Dressing

(About 1½ cups)

Lime juice is the secret.

½ cup lime juice

About 1 square inch outer peel of lime

¼ teaspoon Worcestershire

¼ teaspoon mustard

¼ teaspoon salt

¼ teaspoon paprika

⅓ cup sugar

1 cup salad oil

Blend until smooth. So good with melon salads and fruit-salad plates!

Golden French Dressing

(About 1½ cups)

Serve this with a fruit-salad plate.

1 cup salad oil

Juice 1 orange

Juice 1 lemon
Small piece outer rind of both orange and lemon
½ cup sugar
1 tablespoon vinegar
½ teaspoon salt
1 teaspoon paprika

Blend until smooth.

Spring Salad Dressing

(Around a pint)

As good for mixed greens as for fruit salads.

1 peeled seeded grapefruit, in pieces
½ cup salad oil
3 tablespoons tarragon vinegar
1 tablespoon sugar
1 teaspoon prepared mustard
1 teaspoon paprika
½ teaspoon salt
3 tablespoons catsup
1 small onion, quartered
1 lemon, pared and seeded, in quarters

Blend until smooth.

CREAM, SOUR CREAM AND OTHER DAIRY FOOD DRESSINGS

Sour cream is one of the finest salad dressings of all, and needs but the simplest of seasonings. It is as good with fruit salads as with greens, and I consider it almost indispensable for potato salad, in combination with mayonnaise or cooked dressings. Yogurt gives you the same fine, tart flavor and smooth texture, though it's a little thinner in consistency, with fewer calaries. Cottage cheese converts to sour-cream texture in a blender, and if calories are a problem, you couldn't do better.

Cole Slaw Cream Dressing

(About 2 cups)

You could serve this with ham, as a sauce.

1 cup whipping cream
1 egg
2 tablespoons horse-radish
2 teaspoons prepared mustard
1 teaspoon salt
½ teaspoon sugar
¼ teaspoon paprika
2 tablespoons lemon juice

Blend until thick and smooth.

Cottage Cheese Dressing with Buttermilk

(About 1 cup)

Beloved by weight-watchers.

½ cup cottage cheese
½ cup buttermilk
¼ cup lemon juice
1 teaspoon salt
½ teaspoon paprika
3 hard-cooked egg yolks
   Sliver garlic
½ green pepper, cut in pieces
4 radishes

Blend until green pepper and radishes are finely chopped, not until they are minced too fine to show in the dressing. Awfully good on greens.

Cucumber Sour Cream Dressing

(About 1 ½ cups)

Excellent on pineapple.

1 cup dairy sour cream

    1 tablespoon lemon juice
    ½ teaspoon salt (or more)
    1 cup diced cucumber (leave skin on)
    ¼ teaspoon paprika
      Dash garlic salt or 1 thin sliver garlic

Blend until smooth.

Quick Sour Cream Dressing

(A little over a cup)

Try it on cucumbers and tomato salad.

    1 cup dairy sour cream
    ¼ cup lemon juice
    2 tablespoons sugar
    1 teaspoon salt
      Dash cayenne
      Sprig of parsley (optional)

Blend until smooth and fluffy and use to dress vegetable or fruit salads.

Sour Cream Horse-radish Dressing

(About 2 cups)

Sharp, but refreshing!

    1 cup dairy sour cream
    ¼ cup fresh prepared horse-radish
    ½ cup catsup
    2 tablespoons salad oil
    2 tablespoons vinegar or lemon juice
    2 tablespoons sugar
    1 teaspoon salt

Beat in the blender until smooth. Good on cole slaw and fish salads, especially. Also fine for greens.

Sour Cream Shrimp Dressing
(About 2 cups)

Lobster or crab meat is good in it, too.

1 cup dairy sour cream
1 thin sliver garlic
¼ cup catsup
1 tablespoon Worcestershire
1 slice medium-sized onion
1 tablespoon horse-radish
1 tablespoon lemon juice
½ teaspoon salt
¼ teaspoon mustard
½ teaspoon paprika
¼ pound cooked or canned shrimp

Blend smooth and serve on crisp greens.

Yogurt Dressing
(Little over a cupful)

Sometimes it's spelled yogourt or yoghurt.

1 cup yogurt
1 teaspoon sugar
½ teaspoon salt
Dash pepper
¼ teaspoon mustard
¼ teaspoon paprika
2 tablespoons chili sauce or catsup

Whirl in the blender until thoroughly combined.

MAYONNAISE AND SIMILAR DRESSINGS

The Mayonnaise you make in the blender is the smoothest, fluffiest, most wonderful stuff. And it's perfectly emulsified in nothing flat! Mayonnaise is the base of innumerable fine dressings in addition to being an excellent one all by itself, and many fine sauces for meat and fish begin with a Mayonnaise base. Some of them are included here since they function as dressing or sauce equally well.

Mayonnaise

(A pint or so)

You'll make this a thousand times.

Put into the blender container
>   1 egg
>   1 teaspoon salt
>   1 teaspoon sugar
>   1 teaspoon mustard
>   ½ teaspoon paprika
>   3 tablespoons vinegar or lemon juice

Cover, switch on the motor for just a few seconds, then uncover
and add gradually, with the motor running
>   1½ cups salad oil

Blend until very thick and smooth.

Cheese Mock Mayonnaise

(About 1 ¾ cups)

*Looks and tastes like mayonnaise; cheese makes
it delectable.*

>   ⅔ cup sweetened condensed milk (½ can)
>   ¼ cup vinegar or lemon juice
>   ¼ cup salad oil
>   1 egg yolk
>   ½ teaspoon salt
>   Few grains cayenne pepper
>   1 teaspoon mustard
>   ¼ pound Cheddar cheese, cut in pieces

Blend until smooth and thick. Good on fish as well as for salads
of many kinds. Skip the cheese for just a mock mayonnaise.

Almond Mayonnaise

Try this with Waldorf salad.

Add 1 tablespoon lemon juice and 2 tablespoons Almond Paste
(page 243) to 1 cup Mayonnaise (page 206), and blend.

Caviar Dressing

(A little over a cup)

Don't use the best caviar for this—it's good with the cheapest!

1 cup Mayonnaise (page 206)
1 small stalk celery with tops
1 pimiento
½ green pepper, in pieces
½ small onion
2 tablespoons lemon juice
3 drops tabasco sauce
1 tablespoon red or black caviar

Blend until smooth. This can double as a sauce for fish and sea food.

Cranberry Mayonnaise

(1 ½ cups)

Pale pink and perfect for fruit salads.

½ cup cooked or canned cranberry sauce
½ cup Mayonnaise (page 206)
½ cup sour cream

Blend until smooth. You could spike it with horse-radish, but it's very nice as is.

Cucumber Dressing

(Around 1 ½ cups)

Fine for cold salmon.

1 cup Mayonnaise (page 206)
2 tablespoons chili sauce
1 tablespoon vinegar
½ teaspoon salt
¼ teaspoon pepper
6 pitted green olives or 6 stuffed olives
1 stalk celery, cut up, with tops
1 cucumber, unpared, in pieces

Blend until solid ingredients are chopped fairly fine, but not until you get a smooth sauce. This is good with greens, vegetable salads or as a sauce for cold fish.

Green Goddess Dressing

(A "heaping" pint)

Good on sea food or greens.

1 cup Mayonnaise (page 206)
1 clove garlic
4 anchovies
6 green onions with tops, cut in pieces
¼ cup parsley, packed in cup
1 tablespoon lemon juice
1 tablespoon tarragon vinegar
½ teaspoon salt
¼ teaspoon coarse-ground pepper

Blend until anchovies, onions and parsley are in fine particles. Mix with sweet or sour whipped cream to serve.

Lamaze Dressing or Sauce

(More than a pint)

Almost a relish.

1 cup Mayonnaise (page 206)
1 cup chili sauce or catsup
¼ cup piccalilli or India relish
1 pimiento
1 stalk celery, cut in pieces
1 slice green pepper
1 slice onion
1 tablespoon Worcestershire sauce
1 teaspoon mustard

Blend until solids are in fine particles. My family loves this mixed with yogurt or sour cream, on green salad. It's an elegant sauce for cold salmon and other fish, too.

Parisian Dressing

(1 pint)

Sophisticated.

½ teaspoon mustard
½ teaspoon salt
   Dash white pepper
¼ cup red-wine vinegar
 1 egg
 2 green onions, with tops, in pieces
   Thin sliver garlic
 2 hard-cooked egg yolks
½ bunch water cress
Blend about 30 seconds, then add gradually
 1½ cups salad oil
Blend to smooth, thick emulsion.

Roquefort Mayonnaise

(Around a cupful)

For chicken and fish salads, mostly.

½ cup Mayonnaise (page 206)
⅓ cup Roquefort or blue cheese
 1 medium-sized pickle, cut up
 6 stuffed olives
 5 or 6 sprigs parsley
 1 tablespoon lemon juice
   Dash tabasco sauce
Blend until mixed, but leave fine pieces.

Thousand Island Dressing

(1 pint)

For head lettuce, chicken.

 1 cup Mayonnaise (page 206)
¼ cup chili sauce or catsup
 1 slice onion

¾ cup diced celery
¼ cup stuffed olives
¼ cup sweet pickle relish
2 or 3 sprigs parsley
1 slice green pepper
1 hard-cooked egg, quartered
1 teaspoon paprika

Blend, but not until smooth. Solids should only be chopped.

COOKED SALAD DRESSINGS

The procedure for cooked dressings is to blend first, then cook. Such dressings are smooth as can be.

Old-Fashioned Cooked Dressing

(1 ½ cups)

Better than grandma's!

2 tablespoons flour
1½ teaspoons salt
1 teaspoon mustard
2 tablespoons sugar
¼ teaspoon paprika
1 egg
1¼ cups milk
⅓ cup vinegar

Blend thoroughly, pour into saucepan and cook over hot water until thick. Stir while cooking. Add
1 tablespoon butter

Cole Slaw Dressing

(1 pint)

Good on any greens.

2 eggs
½ cup sugar
1½ teaspoons salt
⅛ teaspoon pepper

1 cup sweet or sour cream
½ cup vinegar
1 teaspoon celery seed

Blend smooth, then cook in a double boiler to smooth **custard.**

Golden Dressing

(About 1 pint)

For fruit salads.

¼ cup sirup from canned fruit (peaches, pears,
     pineapple)
¼ cup orange juice
2 tablespoons lemon juice
¼ teaspoon salt
¼ teaspoon dry mustard
   Few grains cayenne pepper
2 eggs
½ cup sugar

Blend smooth, then cook in the top of a double boiler until **custardy,** stirring constantly.

12

Sauces Smooth as Silk

It's extinct—that lumpy white sauce. It's gone—that bumpy gravy. The electric blender prevents the formation of lumps by perfectly combining liquid and thickener, and it magically unlumps a ruffian sauce made carelessly the old way.

Blend first, then cook, is the general rule. It's a time-saving, sure method. Here's just one example of the new speed and efficiency with which you can prepare a dish: for scalloped potatoes, blend milk, flour, seasonings, pour over the sliced potatoes, without the step of cooking the sauce until thickened. It thickens as the casserole bakes, and with nary a lump or curdle.

WHITE OR CREAM SAUCE AND SOME VARIATIONS

Medium White Sauce

(1 cup)

Use this for all creamed dishes.

> 1 cup milk
> 2 tablespoons flour
> ½ teaspoon salt
> Dash of pepper

Blend ingredients smooth and pour over dish to be baked; or turn into a saucepan and cook, stirring constantly until thickened. Add

> 2 tablespoons butter

Thick or Thin White Sauce

Thick White Sauce is used as the base for croquettes and meat, fish, chicken or vegetable rings, sometimes with the addition of eggs. It also is the base of most soufflés. It is the glue that sticks these things together, and it is very simply made in the blender by just increasing the flour to double the amount—4 tablespoons. Almost always, you'll want to turn the mixture into a saucepan, then, and cook it by itself until thickened. Thin White Sauce is the base for cream soups, and it is made by cutting the flour in half—1 tablespoon of flour to a cup of milk.

Caper Sauce for Fish

Blend an egg yolk with Medium White Sauce and cook and stir until thickened. Then add 1 tablespoon capers and 1 teaspoon lemon juice.

Onion, Parsley and Pimiento Sauce

Blend a slice of onion, 2 or 3 sprigs of parsley, a drained pimiento with the Medium White Sauce. Wonderful for vegetables, cooked chicken or fish.

Good Gravy

There are two kinds of gravy: (1) pan gravy, which is simply drippings from meat which has been broiled, pan-broiled or roasted, minus excess fat and plus enough water to loosen the good meat particles that have browned and attached themselves to the pan, and (2) thickened meat gravy which is simply a white sauce made with water in place of milk. For each cup of thickened gravy put 2 tablespoons flour and a cup of water into the blender, give the mixture a fast whirl and turn into the pan drippings after removing excess fat. If the drippings are good and brown, you'll get brown gravy without browning the flour—and the blender method is antilump. Also, it enables you to cut down on the fat in your gravy if you wish. The old way, you had to use 2 tablespoons fat to 2 tablespoons flour to get a solid foundation for your gravy.

SOME SAUCES FOR MEATS, FISH, POULTRY AND VEGETABLES

For some others, see Mayonnaise and Similar Dressings, pages 205-210 and Entrees, pages 163-179.

Barbecue Sauce

(1 ½ cups)

Just spicy enough.

Quarter, then sauté
        1 medium-sized onion in
          ½ cup butter or margarine
Turn into the blender container and add
        1 tablespoon prepared mustard
        ½ cup vinegar
        1 tablespoon Worcestershire sauce
        1-inch-square outer peel of lemon
        ¼ cup chili sauce
        2 tablespoons brown sugar
        1 teaspoon salt
        ¼ teaspoon pepper
Blend until onion is finely chopped. Use to baste meat or chicken during roasting. Sauce can be "hottened" with tabasco sauce, but be cautious.

Jiffy Cheese Sauce

(2 cups)

Extraordinary!

        1 can condensed cream-of-celery soup
        ⅓ cup sauterne
        ½ pound Cheddar cheese, in cubes
        ½ teaspoon Worcestershire sauce
        2 tablespoons flour
          Salt, pepper
Blend smooth and stir over low heat until thoroughly hot and thickened. Serve over vegetables or over poached eggs.

Creole Sauce for Fish, Meat or Vegetables

(1 pint)

The Spanish cook's stand-by.

Dice and cook for 5 minutes
      1 medium-sized onion
      ½ green pepper in
         ¼ cup butter or margarine
Put in blender with
      1½ cups canned tomatoes
      1 sliver garlic
      1 teaspoon salt
      1 teaspoon sugar
      Dash of black pepper
Blend until vegetables are chopped. Don't overdo this and make them too fine. Heat and serve with fish or other food. Shrimp, frozen fillets of almost any fish are especially good in this sauce. It can be more highly seasoned if you like.

Cucumber Lemon Sauce

(1 ½ cups)

Pale green and so refreshing!

    2 medium-sized cucumbers, cut in pieces
      (don't pare)
     Juice of 1 lemon
     1 teaspoon salt
    ¼ teaspoon paprika
Blend until cucumber is finely grated. Good with fish. Sauce can be combined with Mayonnaise (page 206) or sour cream if you wish.

Cumberland Sauce for Duck or Chicken

(1 cup)

Perfect poultry partner.

    Outer peel of 1 orange, in pieces
    ½ cup currant jelly

> ¼ cup port wine
> ¼ cup orange juice
> 2 tablespoons lemon juice
> 2 teaspoons dry mustard
> 1 teaspoon paprika
> ½ teaspoon ground ginger
> 1 teaspoon cornstarch

Blend until orange rind is finely cut, pour into saucepan and simmer, stirring constantly, for 5 minutes.

Garlic Sauce

(About ⅔ cup)

Gives hamburgers or steaks a snap.

> 1 clove garlic
> 2 tablespoons butter
> ¼ cup catsup
> ¼ cup vinegar
> 1 tablespoon Worcestershire sauce
> 1 teaspoon paprika
> ½ teaspoon dry mustard
> 2 drops tabasco sauce

Blend about 20 seconds and serve with meat.

Gingersnap Sauce

(1 ½ cups)

For ham, tongue or pot roast.

Place in blender

> 5 gingersnaps
> 1 slice onion
> ½ cup brown sugar
> 1 cup hot water
> 1 thick slice lemon

Blend smooth; turn into saucepan and add

> ¼ cup raisins
> ¼ cup vinegar

Cook until thickened.

Hollandaise Sauce

(1 ½ cups)

Nothing like it for green vegetables!

   2 eggs
  ½ teaspoon salt
   2 tablespoons lemon juice
  ½ cup soft butter
     Dash of white pepper (or black)
   1 thin slice onion (optional)
     Sliver garlic (optional)
Blend until smooth, and with motor running, add gradually
  ½ cup hot water
Blend smooth again and then cook over hot water, stirring constantly, to custard consistency. Can be served hot or cold over vegetables. Blend a handful of spinach or water cress with this for green hollandaise—wonderful with fish.

Spaghetti Sauce with Wine

(Enough to serve 6)

Good on rice or noodles, too.

Sauté
   2 onions, quartered in
    ¼ cup olive oil
Turn into blender with
   1 cup red wine
   1 small can mushrooms
   1 clove garlic
Blend until onion is finely chopped and turn into saucepan with
   1 pound hamburger, browned in skillet after onions
   1 cup more red wine
   1 can tomato paste
   2 cups canned tomatoes
  1½ teaspoons salt (more, if needed)
   ¼ teaspoon pepper
Simmer until sauce is heavy, about an hour.

DESSERT SAUCES

Apricot or Peach Rum Sauce

(A little more than a pint)

Serve hot on steamed puddings; cold on angel cake.

    1 No. 2½ can apricots or peaches, drained
    ¼ cup liquid from fruit
    1 tablespoon lemon juice
    ⅓ cup sugar
    1 tablespoon cornstarch
    ¼ teaspoon salt

Blend until fruit is puréed; pour into saucepan and cook, stirring constantly, until thickened and clear. Add

    ¼ cup light rum
       Few drops almond or vanilla extract
    2 tablespoons butter (optional; omit if sauce
        is to be used cold)

Try this on Wonder Sponge Cake (page 47), hot on Plain Two-Egg Cake (page 44), cold on blanc mange, or on a good vanilla ice cream. Pretty fancy!

Brandy Hard Sauce

(Enough for 6 desserts)

The perfect topper for a Christmas pudding.

    2 tablespoons brandy (or rum or sherry)
    ¼ teaspoon nutmeg
    ⅓ cup soft butter
    1 cup confectioners' sugar

Blend until smooth.

Cardamon Wine Sauce

(1 ½ cups)

This is that "something different."

    ½ cup honey

½ cup water
½ teaspoon salt
 6 mint leaves or ½ teaspoon dried mint
 3 peeled cardamon pods
 1 tablespoon lemon juice
 2 teaspoons cornstarch

Blend until cardamon seeds are crushed fine, pour into saucepan and cook and stir until slightly thickened and clear. Cool and add

½ cup sherry, Madeira or other sweet wine

Serve this unusual sauce over fresh fruit, for dessert. Cantaloupe and honeydew balls and blueberries make a wonderful combination "to sauce" with it. The cardamon looks a little like pepper in the finished sauce, but I prefer not to strain it out.

Rich, Thick Chocolate Sauce

(Nearly a cup)

No cooking! Imagine!

 2 squares unsweetened chocolate, cut in small pieces
½ cup sugar
 6 tablespoons warm milk, cream, coffee or sherry
½ teaspoon vanilla
   Dash of salt

Blend until smooth. This is a luscious sauce. Use it for ice cream, pudding, for frosting a cake, flavoring malted milk. Keep it, if you can keep it at all, in the refrigerator.

Custard Sauce with Almonds

(Around a pint)

Nice on a date pudding.

½ cup milk
½ cup blanched almonds
¼ cup sugar
   Dash of salt

Blend until almonds are chopped. Add and blend just a second or two

>2 eggs
>
>1½ cups more milk

Pour into saucepan or double-boiler top and cook and stir over hot water until mixture will just coat a spoon. Add

>¼ teaspoon almond extract

Chill immediately. Serve over plain cake, baked or steamed puddings.

Lemon Sauce

(1 ½ cups)

Your favorite and mine.

>½ cup sugar
>
>1 cup warm water
>
>1 tablespoon cornstarch
>
>Dash of salt
>
>Dash of nutmeg
>
>Juice ½ lemon
>
>Outer peel of ½ lemon

Blend until lemon peel is finely grated; pour into saucepan and cook, stirring constantly, until thickened and clear. Add

>1 tablespoon butter

Serve warm on Plain Two-Egg Cake, page 44 (this combination makes cottage pudding), or on bread pudding or steamed pudding.

Mincemeat Brandy Sauce

(1 ½ cups)

Rich, dark and heavy.

>1 cup canned mincemeat
>
>¼ cup apple juice or orange juice
>
>¼ cup brandy

Give these ingredients a nice whirl to make a smooth sauce which has "oomph" and then some. Serve it cold on ice cream, hot on puddings.

Orange Honey Butter

(1 ½ cups)

For gingerbread, waffles or a stack of "wheats."

¼ cup honey
3 tablespoons frozen orange-juice concentrate
¼ pound butter, soft (½ cup or 1 stick)
6 tablespoons confectioners' sugar
Blend until smooth and creamy.

Raspberry Sauce with Kirsch

(Around 1 ¼ cups)

Tee-riffic!

12-ounce glass raspberry jelly
¼ cup kirsch or cherry brandy
3 or 4 slices outer rind of orange
Blend until rind is finely grated and sauce is smooth. This is potent but perfect for any number of desserts, particularly the light-colored ones (custard, blanc mange, Russian cream) where the color contrast as well as the flavor is interesting.

Strawberry Marshmallow Sauce

(Over a pint)

A pink fluff.

1 box (12 ounce) frozen strawberries, thawed
    slightly and broken up
¼ cup fruit juice or sirup from canned fruit
¼ pound marshmallows, quartered
Blend until smooth. Perfect as an ice-cream topping or parfait sauce.

13 | Soups

The Mock Turtle's soup of the evening could have been no richer and greener than the soup you can turn out of your blender, using peas or asparagus, broccoli, spinach or water cress. Purée any cooked vegetable in your blender, with milk or stock and a piece of onion, turn it into a saucepan, season and heat to the bubbling point. It's smooth, delicious soup, and no straining necessary! A cooked vegetable is its own thickener. You may need to dilute it with milk or stock, but you rarely need to thicken it.

You can make amazingly good soups with all the scraps from your refrigerator. This is a favorite trick of mine, and my family thinks each soup is better than the last. A dab of creamed dried beef, the leftover breakfast bacon, a hunk of mashed potatoes from last night, the little dish of corn and peas—swung together in the blender, with some onion, parsley and milk, these bits of perfectly good food that might otherwise be wasted become a substantial lunch. Blend, heat and eat! Was there ever a simpler recipe?

The Flavor Is Fresher

For really fresh flavor, start with a raw vegetable and chop it fine in the blender, with part of the liquid—milk or stock—you plan to use. Add thickening, too, since a chopped vegetable usually requires thickening. Cooking time for a soup made from a blender-chopped raw vegetable is very short, and thus the fresh flavor is preserved.

Pattern for a Cream Soup Made in the Blender

(2 servings)

Make it with one vegetable or a mixture.

1 cup diced raw vegetable
1 teaspoon salt
Dash of pepper
2 tablespoons flour
2 cups milk
1 slice onion
Sprig or 2 parsley (optional)

Blend until vegetable is chopped, turn into saucepan and heat until thickened, stirring as mixture cooks. If you use greens, allow only the 5 minutes needed for thickening. Firmer vegetables may be cooked in the soup up to 10 minutes. Avoid violent boiling. Add butter, 1 or 2 tablespoons, before serving soup.

Soups with Stock, Not Milk

Use the same pattern for soups from meat stock, substituting the stock for milk and cutting down the seasonings if the stock is seasoned. Use 2 bouillon cubes and 2 cups water, or a can of consommé diluted with a can of water if you haven't any meat stock.

Almond Soup

(4 servings)

Rich and aristocratic.

Sauté in a little butter until pale brown
1 cup blanched almonds
Turn into the blender container and add
1 cup chicken stock or bouillon
¼ teaspoon dry mustard
¼ teaspoon paprika
½ teaspoon sugar
1 tablespoon flour

Switch on the motor and blend until almonds have been cut
very fine. Turn into saucepan and add
>   2 more cups chicken stock
Heat about 15 minutes and add
>   1 cup cream
Serve as soon as hot. You don't need to sauté the almonds, but
if you like a toasty, buttery flavor, I recommend it. Or you can
brown half of them in butter and leave the rest plain.

Avocado Soup

(4 servings)

Party stuff, and so easy!

Blend until smooth
>   1 large avocado, diced
>   1 cup cream
Heat in saucepan
>   2 cups well-seasoned chicken stock
Add avocado and cream and barely heat through. Garnish with
whipped cream. If you have an extra avocado, dice some of it
into your soup bowls. You might run whipped-cream topped
soup bowls under the broiler flame for a minute if the pottery
can take heat. Half clam broth and half chicken broth turns
this into an epicure's dream, especially if you add 2 tablespoons
of sherry at the last. And the soup can be served cold, too!

Beet Borsch

(4 servings)

A genuine appetizer.

Place in blender container
>   1 cup pared, diced raw beets
>   1 small onion, quartered
>   1 cup diced potato
>   1 cup chicken or beef stock or bouillon
Blend until vegetables are chopped. Turn into saucepan with
>   1 tablespoon lemon juice

1 teaspoon sugar
  Dash of celery salt
1 cup more stock
  Salt, pepper to taste

Simmer 10 minutes to blend flavors. Serve cold or hot with sour cream on top.

Buttermilk Soup

(3 servings)

Chilly, with a tang you'll like.

2 cups buttermilk
1 egg
2 tablespoons sugar
½ teaspoon vanilla
  Juice ½ lemon

Blend a few seconds and serve cold.

Lobster Buttermilk Soup

(For 4)

Fresh herbs make all the difference!

Place in blender container

½ cup cooked or canned lobster meat or shrimp
1 small cucumber, diced
½ bunch water cress
1 spray fresh dill, cut in pieces
1 teaspoon prepared mustard
1 teaspoon sugar
2 cups buttermilk

Whirl these ingredients in your blender until everything's in fine particles, then add

1 cup more buttermilk
  Salt to taste

Serve chilly, topped with freshly clipped chives.

Carrot Cream Soup with Cheese

(4 or 5 servings)

Has palate appeal.

Blend until grated, then set aside
> ½ cup diced hard (natural) Cheddar cheese

Place in blender container
> 2 cups milk
> 1 slice medium-sized onion
> 4 medium-sized carrots, cut in chunks
> 5 sprigs parsley
> ¼ cup flour
> 1¼ teaspoons salt
> ¼ teaspoon pepper

Switch on motor and let it run until carrots are finely chopped but not liquefied. Turn into saucepan and add
> 2 cups more milk

Cook and stir until thickened. Stir in
> 3 tablespoons butter
> The grated cheese

Serve at once. This soup has a really fresh carrot flavor because of the brief cooking.

Cherry Soup

(3 servings)

A little spice, and very nice!

> 2 cups pitted fresh or canned cherries, sweet or sour, with their juice and ½ cup water
> ½ cup orange juice
> Outer peel of ½ orange
> Dash of salt
> ¼ teaspoon cinnamon
> ⅓ cup sugar (more for tart cherries)
> 1 tablespoon cornstarch

Blend until cherries are finely chopped, pour into saucepan and cook and stir until clear-looking. Chill and serve with whipped-cream topping. You'll have to taste and estimate the sugar for yourself. It varies a lot with the kind of cherries used.

Chestnut and Squash Soup

(4 servings)

Decidedly different, and decidedly delicious, too!

Boil for 5 minutes, then remove outer shell and peel of
>½ pound chestnuts

Sauté in 2 tablespoons butter
>¼ cup diced onion
>¼ cup sliced celery
>¼ cup sliced carrot

Add chestnuts and the following ingredients
>1 bay leaf
>1½ cups beef stock
>1½ teaspoons sugar

Simmer until chestnuts are soft. Remove bay leaf. Cool somewhat, then place in blender container with
>1 cup cooked squash

Blend until ingredients are smooth. Pour back into saucepan and add
>½ cup cream

If the soup seems thick, dilute with more stock. Add salt if you need it, and serve garnished with whipped cream and cut chives.

Curry Soup

(4 servings)

For particular people.

Cook together gently for 10 minutes
>¼ cup butter
>1 large, sliced sweet onion

Cool somewhat, then transfer to blender and add
>2½ cups beef, veal or chicken stock or bouillon
>1 teaspoon curry powder
>¼ teaspoon ginger
>¼ teaspoon nutmeg
>2 tablespoons flour
>1 egg

Blend smooth, turn into saucepan and cook gently until thick and smooth. Add

> 1 cup cream
> 2 tablespoons sherry

Heat gently, but do not boil.

Green Pepper Meat Soup

(6 servings)

Substantial lunch.

Place in blender container

> 2 large green peppers, cut in pieces
> 1 large onion, diced
> 2 cups canned tomatoes
> 2 slices half-cooked bacon, diced

Blend until ingredients are chopped, but not too fine. Place in saucepan with

> 1 quart meat stock or consommé
> 1 pound hamburger
> Salt and pepper as needed

Cover pan and bring to boil; reduce heat and simmer for 1 hour.

Mushroom Cream Soup

(3 servings)

The richest, but surely the best, you've ever eaten!

Cook together for 5 minutes

> ½ pound washed, dried mushrooms (*fresh* ones)
> ¼ pound (1 stick) butter

Cool and turn into the blender container with

> 2 cups chicken stock

Blend until mushrooms are coarsely chopped and add

> 3 egg yolks

Blend just a second or two and turn into a saucepan with 1 cup cream. Stir and heat gently until thickened. Season, if necessary, with salt and pepper.

Olive Soup

(6 servings)

This unusual soup has a piquancy you'll enjoy.

Cook together gently for 5 minutes
>3 tablespoons butter
>1 onion, quartered
>6 ribs celery, in ½-inch pieces

Cool and turn into blender container with
>½ cup pimiento-stuffed olives
>½ cup flour
>1½ cups water
>2 teaspoons salt
>½ teaspoon pepper

Blend until vegetables are chopped fairly fine. Turn into saucepan and add
>½ cup water
>2 cups milk

Cook over low heat until smooth and thickened. If the soup seems thick, add a little more water or milk.

Fresh Pea Soup

(4 servings)

Made with lettuce, the French way.

Place in blender container
>½ cup parsley
>½ small head lettuce, cut in pieces
>1 cup bouillon

Blend until parsley and lettuce are fine, then turn into saucepan and add
>½ package frozen peas or 1 cup fresh peas
>1½ more cups bouillon
>1 tablespoon butter

Cook gently 5 minutes or until peas are tender. Garnish with sour cream.

Pimiento Cream Soup

(6 servings)

Pretty color; interesting flavor.

Place in blender container
>>> ¼ cup parsley
>>> 4 pimientos and juice
>>> 1 slice onion
>>> 3 tablespoons flour
>>> 2 cups milk
>>> 1 egg

Blend these ingredients until parsley is finely chopped, and pour into saucepan with
>>> 3 cups more milk
>>> ¼ cup chili sauce
>>> 1 teaspoon salt

Cook and stir until thickened and serve topped with paprika.

Potato Cheese Soup

(4 servings)

Plain, common, good!

Cook together 10 minutes
>>> 1 cup diced potatoes
>>> 1 bouillon cube
>>> 2 cups water

Cool and turn into blender container with
>>> 1 slice onion
>>> 5 or 6 sprigs parsley
>>> 1 cup diced Cheddar or Swiss cheese
>>> 2 tablespoons flour

Blend a few seconds and turn into saucepan used to cook potatoes. Add
>>> 1 cup milk or cream
>>> Salt, pepper to taste
>>> Dash of Worcestershire sauce

Cook gently, stirring constantly, until soup thickens. Thin it with more milk, if you need to, before serving. You can make a very unusual soup of this by using a wedge of Roquefort-type cheese (about 3 ounces) in place of the cheese suggested.

Scandinavian Fruit Soup

(6 or more servings)

This one can precede or follow the entree.

Cook together until tender

      ½ pound dried prunes, pitted
      ½ pound dried apricots
      3 apples, cored and diced
      ½ cup sugar
      1½ quarts water or fruit juice and water
      1 stick cinnamon

Remove cinnamon and purée the fruits in your blender (not all at once), being sure to cool the mixture sufficiently first so that you won't break the glass. Return fruits to saucepan and add

      2 tablespoons cornstarch mixed with a little
          cold water

Cook and stir until clear-looking. Chill and serve very cold. Can be flavored with port wine—about a tablespoonful per serving.

Spinach Curry Soup

(6 servings)

A green smoothie.

Place in blender container

      ½ pound fresh spinach
      2 tablespoons flour
      2 cups stock or water
      2 teaspoons curry powder

Blend ingredients until spinach is very fine. Turn into saucepan and add

      2 tall cans (3½ cups) evaporated milk
      Salt to taste

Cook just until thickened, stirring to keep smooth.

Fresh Tomato Cream Soup

(4 servings)

No curdle; fresh flavor.

Place in blender container
> 2 cups milk
> ½ teaspoon salt
> 1 tablespoon flour

Blend a few seconds, then cook in saucepan until thickened, stirring constantly. Meanwhile, put into blender container
> 4 medium-sized, ripe tomatoes, coarse-diced
> 3 sprigs parsley
> 1 teaspoon sugar
> Sprinkle of cloves
> 2 slices onion
> ½ teaspoon salt
> ¼ teaspoon pepper

Whirl until smooth and add tomato purée gradually to hot white sauce, stirring constantly. Serve as soon as thoroughly hot, with sour cream or whipped cream on top. Be sure to taste the soup for seasonings. You may need a little more salt.

Tomato Oyster Bisque

(6 servings)

An "R" season favorite.

Pick over and remove any bits of shell from
> 1 pint oysters

Place in blender container with oyster liquor and
> 1 cup milk

Blend until oysters are chopped fine. Pour into another container. Into blender place
> 1 slice onion
> 1 tablespoon flour
> 2 teaspoons salt
> ¼ teaspoon pepper
> 1 can condensed tomato soup
> 2 cups milk

Blend a few seconds, turn into saucepan and cook, stirring constantly until thickened. Add oysters and
>
> 1 cup cream
> 2 tablespoons butter

Serve as soon as hot.

Vichysoisse

(4 servings)

Cold elegance.

Cook together gently for 5 minutes
>
> 4 big leeks, sliced (use tops, too)
> 3 tablespoons butter

Turn into blender with
>
> 3 medium-sized potatoes, diced
> 2 cups chicken broth

Blend until vegetables are very fine. Pour into saucepan and add
>
> 1 cup more chicken broth
> Salt, white pepper as needed

Cook gently 10 minutes and add
>
> ¾ cup heavy cream

Chill and serve with cut chives on each portion.

Water Cress Soup

(For 4 gourmets)

Full of vitamins, too.

Place in blender container
>
> 1 bunch washed water cress
> 1 tablespoon flour
> 2 cups chicken broth, bouillon or consommé

Blend until cress is finely chopped, turn into saucepan and heat through with
>
> 1 cup cream

Garnish with whipped cream, sprinkle with paprika.

14 | Vegetables

At first thought you might dismiss the electric blender as far as vegetables are concerned. But for soufflés and vegetable rings, the blender can reduce a raw or cooked vegetable to the required fine particles. The blender can also prepare the fine crumbs to top a vegetable casserole, the grated cheese for au gratin dishes. It can mince the onion, garlic and green pepper needed to season some vegetable combinations, and help prepare the smooth white-sauce base for others.

Blender-chopped nuts, plain or toasted, dress up a green vegetable like asparagus or broccoli beautifully. After chopping the nuts you can sauté them in a little butter for added "toothsomeness." Cooked chestnuts can be chopped in a blender to dress another vegetable (Brussels sprouts, for example) or puréed entirely if you like them puréed.

Asparagus Casserole

(4 servings)

A pleasing luncheon entree.

Prepare in blender
    1 cup soft bread crumbs (2 slices bread)
Place half the crumbs in greased baking dish. Place alternate layers of the following in baking dish
    1 pound asparagus, cut in 1-inch pieces, cooked
    4 hard-cooked eggs, sliced
    2 pimientos, cut in strips
In blender container place
    2 tablespoons butter
    2 tablespoons flour
    ½ teaspoon salt

1 cup milk
1 cup Cheddar cheese, diced

Blend smooth and pour over asparagus and eggs. Top with remainder of crumbs. Dot with

2 tablespoons butter

Bake in moderate oven, 350°, for 30 minutes.

Burgundy Beans

(6 servings)

Perfect for a winter buffet.

Simmer for an hour

2 cups kidney or pink beans
1 slice salt pork
1 quart water

Place ingredients in a casserole. Place in the blender container

1 large onion, quartered
1 clove garlic
1¼ teaspoons salt
1 8-ounce can tomato sauce
1 tablespoon brown sugar
1 teaspoon dry mustard
¼ cup salad oil
½ teaspoon black pepper

Blend until onion is fine and pour over beans. Mix in

½ pound American cheese, cubed

Cover and bake at 275° for 4 hours, adding in small amounts from time to time

1 cup Burgundy wine

Rum Baked Beans

(6 servings)

Make it sherry, if you don't care for rum. Exotic!

Simmer 2 hours in water to cover

1 pound navy beans
1 ham bone

Drain beans and place in beanpot. Into the blender container put

    1 cup bean liquid
    ½ cup brown sugar
    2 onions, quartered
    1 sliver garlic
  1½ teaspoons salt
    ½ bay leaf
    ¼ teaspoon pepper

Blend until onions are finely chopped. Pour over beans. Add more bean liquid to cover. Cover and bake at 275° about 4 hours. Add the last half hour

    ½ cup rum (or sherry)

I sometimes add a small can of crushed pineapple to these beans.

Piquant Beets

(6 servings)

Beets in a hurry, this dish!

    3 cups pared sliced raw beets
    ¾ cup water
    ¼ cup vinegar (tarragon, if you have it)
    2 tablespoons butter
    1 teaspoon salt
    ⅛ teaspoon pepper
    ½ cup sugar
    2 tablespoons cornstarch

Blend until beets are chopped coarsely. Turn into saucepan and cook and stir over moderate heat about 15 minutes, until thickened and cooked throughout. You can use lemon juice in place of vinegar and add a strip of lemon peel to the ingredients if you'd rather.

Broccoli Loaf

(6 servings)

A main course this way.

Chop in blender cooked broccoli to make
    2 cups chopped broccoli
Turn into pan. Into blender place

2 eggs
1 cup canned tomatoes
1 slice medium-sized onion
1 cup diced celery
3 tablespoons butter
½ teaspoon salt
¼ teaspoon pepper

Blend to chop vegetables. Add to broccoli with

1 cup coarse cracker crumbs

Bake in greased loaf pan at 350°, moderate oven, about 40 minutes. Serve with White Sauce (page 212) or cheese sauce.

Carrot Ring

(4 servings)

Rule for getting Johnny to eat carrots.

Tear into blender container and cut to crumbs

1 slice bread

Set aside. Place in container

3 eggs
1 slice onion
4 sprigs parsley
1 tablespoon melted butter
1 teaspoon salt
¼ teaspoon pepper
2½ cups cooked diced carrots
1 tablespoon maple sirup or brown sugar

Blend until carrots are finely cut. Fold in bread crumbs and turn into a buttered 8-inch ring mold. Set in a shallow pan of water and bake in moderately hot oven, 375°, for 30 minutes or until firm. Unmold on serving plate and fill with creamed peas.

Cauliflower with Crumbs and Nuts

(4 servings)

A quickie with flavor.

Cook until tender, whole or broken apart

1 medium-sized head cauliflower

Break into blender container and cut into fine crumbs
>   1 slice bread
Empty crumbs into saucepan with
>   ¼ cup melted butter
Add
>   ¼ cup nuts (pecans, preferably), ground fine in
>   blender
Brown lightly over moderate heat and pour over the salted and peppered cauliflower.

Corn Pie

(A 9-incher; for 5)

With salad, a good lunch.

Line a 9-inch pie pan with
>   Plain pie pastry (½ recipe or ½ package mix)
Build rim up high. Place in blender container
>   1 cup light cream
>   1 teaspoon salt
>   1 slice green pepper
>   1 slice onion
>   5 sprigs parsley
>   1 egg
Blend about 20 seconds. Add contents of
>   1 No. 2 can cream-style corn
Turn into pastry-lined pie pan. Top with
>   ½ cup buttered crumbs (crumbs can be made
>   in blender with 1 slice bread)
>   ⅓ cup grated cheese
Bake pie in hot oven, 450°, for 10 minutes, then lower heat to 350° for 25 minutes longer or until firm in center.

Nut Stuffed Eggplant

(4 to 6 servings)

So easy to do!

Cook 15 minutes in boiling water
>   1 whole egg plant

Drain, cut in half lengthwise and cut out pulp with a spoon, leaving a shell about ¾ inch thick. Place in blender container

> The scooped out eggplant pulp
> 4 or 5 sprigs parsley
> ¼ medium-sized onion
> 1 egg
> Salt, pepper, dash of marjoram

Switch on motor and let run until ingredients are finely chopped.
Mix with

> ½ cup chopped nuts (can be blender-chopped,
>   you know)
> 2 cups soft bread crumbs (4 slices bread broken
>   into blender, 1 at a time)

Add more salt if you need it and fill eggplant shells. Bake in moderately hot oven, 375°, about 40 minutes, basting occasionally with mixture of

> ¼ cup water
> 2 tablespoons butter

Onion Ring

(6 servings)

So good!

Purée in blender enough half-boiled onions to make

> 1 cup onion purée

Add

> 2 tablespoons butter
> 2 tablespoons flour
> ½ cup milk
> 1 teaspoon salt
> ⅛ teaspoon pepper
> ½ cup diced cheese
> 3 egg yolks

Blend a few seconds and pour into saucepan. Cook over moderate heat, stirring constantly until thickened. Remove from heat and fold in

> 3 egg whites, beaten stiff

Pour into buttered ring mold, set in a pan of hot water and bake in a 350° oven about an hour, or until set. A few sprigs of parsley can be added. Turn the ring onto a hot platter and fill center with buttered peas or another bright-colored vegetable.

Potato Puff

(4 servings)

A new way for potatoes.

4 sizable potatoes, cut in large dice
¼ cup firmly packed parsley
1 onion, cut in dice
½ green pepper, cut in dice
1 cup milk
3 eggs
1½ teaspoons salt
¼ teaspoon pepper
1 cup diced cheese
½ cup butter

Blend all ingredients until potatoes are finely grated and turn into buttered casserole. Bake in 350° oven for about an hour.

Spinach or Carrot Soufflé

(5 servings)

Use this recipe for any vegetable soufflé.

Place in blender container
¾ cup milk
¼ cup soft butter
4 egg yolks
¼ cup flour
1 slice onion
1 teaspoon salt
⅛ teaspoon pepper
½ cup diced cheese
2 cups packed, washed raw spinach or 1½ cups
diced raw carrot

Blend until vegetable is finely cut. Turn into saucepan and cook and stir until thickened over moderate heat. Cool slightly and fold in

4 egg whites, beaten stiff
Turn into greased casserole, sprinkle with paprika and bake in 325° oven 50 minutes to an hour. Serve immediately, by itself or with a tomato or mushroom sauce.

Sweet Potatoes with Bananas

(4 servings)

Tropical treat.

Chop together in blender
　　　⅓ cup toasted almonds
　　　⅓ cup toasted walnuts
Turn into a bowl with
　　　2 cups mashed sweet potatoes (can be blender-
　　　　　mashed)
　　　1 tablespoon sugar
　　　　Pinch of salt
　　　1 tablespoon butter
　　　½ teaspoon vanilla
Crumb in blender
　　　1 slice bread
Add to potatoes. Mash in blender
　　　2 bananas
Mix with potato combination. Shape into small mounds in well-greased pan. Top each mound with
　　　　Walnut half
Bake in a moderate oven, 350°, for 15 minutes.

Orange Baked Yams

(4 servings)

Lots of flavor here.

Place in baking dish
　　　1 can sweet potatoes, sirup-packed, drained of
　　　　　sirup and sliced
　　　2 tablespoons butter
Place in blender container

Sirup from potatoes
Pinch of ginger
Pinch of mace
¼ orange, including peel (no seeds),
    cut in several pieces
¼ teaspoon salt
1 tablespoon brown sugar

Blend until orange is fine. Pour over potatoes and bake at 350°, moderate oven, 1 hour, basting several times with sirup in dish.

Stuffed Baked Tomatoes

(6 servings)

A handsome dish!

Wash and scoop out centers of
    6 large tomatoes
Turn upside down to drain. Place in blender container
    2 cups packed spinach
    1 cup milk
    3 tablespoons flour
    3 tablespoons butter
    ½ cup diced cheese
    ½ teaspoon salt

Blend until spinach is coarsely chopped. Turn into saucepan and cook and stir until thick. Sprinkle tomatoes inside with
    Salt and pepper
Fill with spinach mixture. Top with
    ½ cup soft bread crumbs (1 slice bread, blended)
    ¼ cup grated cheese

Bake in shallow pan at 350°, moderate oven, 15 minutes or until thoroughly hot.

15

Quick Tricks
with a Blender

When you've learned to use your blender for more than drinks and salad dressings you'll discover that it can help you cut time and labor in many different kinds of cooking operations. These are some of the blender's accomplishments.

Almond Paste

(Well over a pint)

For roll and coffee-cake fillings and candies.

Place in blender container
    ½ cup orange juice
    1 cup blanched almonds
    1 cup sugar
Blend until nuts are very fine. Add
    1 cup more almonds
Blend again until nuts are fine. Store this good paste in a covered jar in the refrigerator to use as you want it. For candy centers, work confectioners' sugar into it until it holds shape firmly, then dip in melted chocolate.

Baby Foods

Some blender manufacturers recommend their machines for use in the preparation of strained baby foods. There may be two objections: (1) with only one exception, blenders are not made so that they can be sterilized easily for such use, and (2) strained foods prepared in the blender are not in the true sense strained—they may contain vegetable fibers which might conceivably be upsetting to a tiny baby. Blender-prepared baby foods should be safe after the babe is 6 months old if Mother uses reasonable care. Skip the salt and blend small portions of the family's vegetables for the baby. A blender is very useful in preparing that mashed banana, too.

Grated Coconut

It was always hard work to grate coconut until the advent of the blender. Now you crack the coconut, pick out the meat, pare off the brown part and do your grating in the blender. The process works faster if you cover blender blades with water, coconut water or milk (about ¼ cup), and of course it is important not to do too much at a time. If you want dry grated coconut for a cake, merely drain off the liquid after preparing it. You can toast the drained coconut in a moderate oven, if you like, but spread it out thin on a cooky sheet to do it most successfully.

Frozen or Canned Fruit Juices

The blender is ideal for reconstituting frozen fruit juice. Turn the orange juice or other frozen breakfast drink into the blender, add 2¼ cups water (or 3 cans full) and put the cover on the blender. Switch on, switch off, and there you are! Quick blending improves the flavor of canned citrus juices.

Reconstituting Dry Milk Solids

Bet your family won't know the difference, even for drinking, when you "make" milk in a blender. Use 3 to 4 tablespoons dry milk to 1 cup water.

Preserves, Jams, Conserves

The blender is a reliable masher, chopper and purée-er of fruits for preserving. If you don't insist on paper-thin *sliced* fruit for marmalade, you can save yourself a lot of work by letting the blender chop fine those oranges and lemons.

Whipping Cream into Butter

If by chance you are sometime out of butter but have ½ pint of useless whipping cream sitting around in the refrigerator, give it the whirl of its life. What do you get? Butter! And in a great big hurry, too. You'll find that some blender manufacturers recommend whipping cream by blender, and you may even see some demonstrations of it. But the blender doesn't give you the volume in whipped cream that a rotary beater, electric mixer or cream whipper gives, and whips cream to butter so fast that you may not catch it in time.

Index